The Interpreter's Guidebook

Technique ~~LIBRARY~~ entations

by Kathleen Regnier
Michael Gross and Ron Zimmerman
James Heintzman, Consulting Editor

UW-SP FOUNDATION PRESS, INC.
UNIVERSITY OF WISCONSIN
STEVENS POINT
STEVENS POINT, WI 54481

The Interpreter's Guidebook: Techniques for Programs and Presentations
Third Edition, 1994

ISBN 0-932310-17-6

Library of Congress Catalog Card Number
91-66610

Printed on
Recycled Paper

About the Interpreter's Handbook Series

The Interpreter's Guidebook: Techniques for Programs and Presentations

The second in a series of practical guides for interpretive professionals and students. Other topics in the series are:

Making the Right Connections: A Guide for Nature Writers

Creating Environmental Publications: A Guide to Writing and Designing for Interpreters and Environmental Educators

Signs, Trails, and Wayside Exhibits: Connecting People and Places

For more information, contact:

Dr. Michael Gross
College of Natural Resources
University of Wisconsin-Stevens Point
Stevens Point, WI 54481

Cover photo: Yellowstone National Park, Wyoming, by Alan Leftridge
Inside cover: Point Reyes National Seashore, California, by Donna Zimmerman

Kathleen Regnier
Seasonal Naturalist at The Ridges Sanctuary
and full-time Elementary School Teacher
Baileys Harbor, WI 54202

Michael Gross
Professor of Environmental Interpretation
College of Natural Resources
University of Wisconsin
Stevens Point, WI 54481

Ron Zimmerman
Director, Schmeeckle Reserve
Instructor of Environmental Interpretation
College of Natural Resources
University of Wisconsin
Stevens Point, WI 54481

Contents

Acknowledgements

Many of our colleagues offered insights and helpful suggestions to improve this revision of the *Nature Fakir's Handbook*. Tom Danton of The National Park Service wrote much of Chapter One, providing an historical perspective for our profession. Dave Imbrogno of the Cincinnati Museum contributed personal reflections on Warren and Elizabeth Wells.

Storytelling techniques were enthusiastically shared by Susan Gilchrist, Wisconsin Department of Natural Resources. A spectrum of puppetry techniques were made possible by photos and ideas from Marti Kane, North Carolina Wildlife Resources Commission, Beth Heidorn, Minnesota Zoo, Dr. Pat Rutowski, Monterey Bay Aquarium, and Connie Lee Potratz Watson of St. Croix National Scenic Riverway.

Three friends and colleagues were asked for photos and ideas for this new edition. Their photos are found throughout. Warren Bielenberg, National Park Service, Sandy Frost, United States Forest Service, and Doug Moore, University of Wisconsin-Stevens Point deserve our heartfelt thanks. Many other photos were contributed by people from various agencies and organizations as cited in the book.

Mike Freed and Dave Shafer graciously granted permission to reproduce their Interpreter's Knapsack list.

Once again, Char Pingel was an indispensable member of the team. She helped edit, design, and proof the pages. Her skill with desktop publishing and dedication to the project makes this series possible.

1
Roots and Reasons

Poetry should begin in entertainment and end in wisdom.
- Robert Frost

Foundations of Interpretation

Enos A. Mills (1870-1922)

Nature guides blazed the trail to modern interpretation as they shared the beauty of the American wilderness with turn of the century adventurers. One of the best known of these early guides was Enos Mills who led excursions into the Rocky Mountains from 1889 until his death in 1922. He is regarded as the founder of the profession we call interpretation.

By his mid-teens, Enos Mills was guiding visitors to the 14,256 foot summit of Longs Peak and to other destinations in the Colorado Rockies. Over the next 35 years, Mills would be known as a naturalist, interpreter, author of 15 books about nature, a lecturer, Father of Rocky Mountain National Park, crusader for parks and preserves, founder of the Trail School (an early version of environmental education programs), and trainer of interpreters.

Mills' insatiable curiosity about nature and his contagious enthusiasm helped make him the ideal nature interpreter, but Mills did not stop there. He carefully analyzed his interpretation with visitors. He noted what techniques worked best and tried to understand why others failed.

Courtesy of Enos Mills Cabin, Longs Peak, Colorado

Courtesy of Enos Mills Cabin, Longs Peak, Colorado

Mills' Trail School introduced visitors to the Rocky Mountains and became a training ground for novice interpreters.

Courtesy of Enos Mills Cabin, Longs Peak, Colorado

Mills was a patient observer of nature. He took seven years to gain the trust of a big horn ram. He studied beaver for twenty-seven years before writing *In Beaver World* in 1913.

He believed his mission as a guide was more than directing people safely through the wilderness. "A nature guide is not a guide in the ordinary sense of the word, and is not a teacher. At all times, however, he is rightfully associated with information and with some form of education. But nature guiding, as we see it, is more inspirational than informational."

"A nature guide (interpreter) is a naturalist who can guide others to the secrets of nature. It is not necessary for a guide to be a walking encyclopedia. He arouses interest by dealing in big principles, -- not with detached and colorless information."

And what about techniques for leading a group in the woods? Mills offered many insights. "The nature guide who understands human nature and possesses tact and ingenuity is able to hold divergent interests and scattering members of his party together. He appreciates, too, the eloquence of silence and is skillful in controlling, directing, and diverting the conversation of members of his party lest the beauty of the outdoors be marred... He is master of the art of suggestion. He is a leader rather than a teacher."

Mills wrote about interpretation as a profession and began teaching its art and science to others. His Trail School introduced visitors to the Rocky Mountains, and became a training ground for many novice interpreters. Under his guiding hand, men and women became patient observers of nature and enthusiastic trail leaders. In 1917, two of Mills' best pupils, Esther and Elizabeth Burnell, were licensed by the National Park Service to conduct interpretive tours in Rocky Mountain National Park.

Before his untimely death in 1922, Enos Mills organized the profession of interpretation. He developed principles, guidelines, and techniques which laid the foundation for modern interpretation.

Without Mills, the new profession meandered. Sometimes parks sought out university professors who lectured visitors without spontaneity or enthusiasm. Inspiration was often sacrificed for scientific accuracy.

By the mid-1950's, Mills' books about the profession had long been out of print. A new book filled the void: *Interpreting Our Heritage* by Freeman Tilden.

Freeman Tilden (1883-1980)

Freeman Tilden was not a renowned naturalist or interpreter, but he possessed impressive experience as a newspaper reporter, playwright, non-fiction author, and keen observer/commentator. In mid-life, Tilden was eager to do something different. The National Park Service invited him to tour the national parks, write about them, and analyze what was happening with interpretation. Tilden accepted the challenge.

Tilden traveled for years, observing ranger walks, talks, and other ways park professionals communicate with visitors. He noted the public's reactions to different styles and media of presentation. Tilden analyzed the practices of a profession much as Mills had done 40 years earlier.

In 1957, *Interpreting Our Heritage* was the first book written solely to define the profession of interpretation. It does not describe how to lead a tour, nor does it list the steps in preparing a talk. *Interpreting Our Heritage* answers the question: why do we interpret? It establishes goals and identifies principles for quality interpretation. The reader discovers a philosophy, an attitude, of interpretation.

In 105 pages, Tilden captured the essence of a profession. The book was officially endorsed by the National Park Service, other federal agencies, numerous state and county parks, museums, and the academic world. The profession returned to the path begun by Mills.

Tilden would spend the next 20 years teaching the art and science of interpretation. His principles are still the most recognized standards for interpretation.

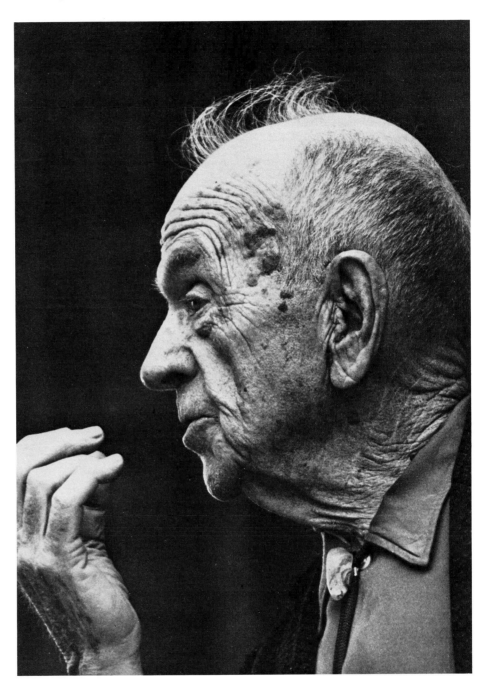

In *Interpreting Our Heritage,* Freeman Tilden defined interpretation as "an educational activity which aims to reveal meanings and relationships through the use of original objects, by firsthand experience, and by illustrative media, rather than simply to communicate factual information."

Two concepts were stated as central to the philosophy of interpretation. "Interpretation is the revelation of a larger truth that lies behind any statement of fact." "Interpretation should capitalize on mere curiosity for the enrichment of the human mind and spirit."

Tilden's Principles of Interpretation

I. Any interpretation that does not somehow relate what is being displayed or described to something within the personality or experience of the visitor will be sterile.

II. Information, as such, is not interpretation. Interpretation is revelation based upon information. But they are entirely different things. However, all interpretation includes information.

III. Interpretation is an art, which combines many arts, whether the materials presented are scientific, historical, or architectural. Any art is in some degree teachable.

IV. The chief aim of interpretation is not instruction, but provocation.

V. Interpretation should aim to present a whole rather than a part, and must address itself to the whole man rather than any phase.

VI. Interpretation addressed to children (say, up to the age of twelve) should not be a dilution of the presentation to adults, but should follow a fundamentally different approach. To be at its best, it will require a separate program.

Tilden saw six principles at the foundation of any interpretive event, whether personal or non-personal. Most of his book is devoted to explaining and illustrating these principles.

Compared to Mills' straight-forward, practical approach to interpretation, Tilden is often deeply philosophical, requiring several readings and personal reflection to understand. The two greatest leaders of interpretation had very contrasting styles to express and explain the same profession. Yet, both Enos Mills and Freeman Tilden are worthy of study by interpreters today.

Quotes for the preceeding biographies were from the following books. We recommend them for every interpreter's library:

Enos A. Mills, *The Adventures of a Nature Guide,* 1920, reprinted in 1990 with additional chapters from other Mills' books, available from New Past Press, Inc., 2098 18th Ave., Friendship, WI 53934

Freeman Tilden, *Interpreting Our Heritage,* 1957, available from the University of North Carolina Press, Chapel Hill, North Carolina.

Point Reyes National Seashore   Donna Zimmerman

A gray whale's size is put into perspective. This interpretation applies the first two principles: relating to visitors' experiences and revealing information in a way they can understand.

Goals of Interpretation

Environmental interpretation becomes even more important as natural landscapes and cultural treasures disappear. Today, the public has an expanding role in land management decisions. Agencies value an informed public capable of supporting and participating in management decisions.

Interpretation serves agency objectives by educating the public. Interpretive programs can shed light on controversial practices like prescribed burning or deer herd reduction. These often misunderstood practices have a sound ecological basis.

Environmental interpretation leads to responsible visitor use of a site. An informed and caring public will not harm a site through vandalism, littering, or thoughtless destruction. Visitors can learn their role in fire prevention, dune conservation, or grizzly bear safety. In a larger sense a concerned public becomes an advocate for the site, supporting elected officials and agency administrators when development threatens.

(handwritten: definition as described in relation to specific sites 'Goals'!)

Goals of Interpretation

As they relate to the Site:
- Foster proper use.
- Develop advocates for the site.

As they relate to the Agency:
- Enhance image of the agency.
- Encourage public participation in management.

As they relate to the Visitor:
- Provide recreation.
- Heighten awareness and understanding of their natural and cultural environment.
- Inspire and add perspective to their lives.

Interpret the Site

Interpreters serve as links between the visitor and the site. Therefore, they must have a thorough knowledge of their area.

They must know the natural and cultural history and understand their universal implications. This requires solid grounding in the sciences and humanities. But even more important is the first-hand knowledge that can be gained only in the field. If you are going to be a spokesperson for the environment, you must know what the environment has to say.

Some sites have subtle messages. A group that has never seen a salt marsh may need a little guidance to appreciate it. Without help from a trained naturalist would they really see the tall cord grass? Would they understand its role in stabilizing rich organic mud, thus assuring survival of other grasses in the upper salt meadows?

Can an uninformed visitor fully understand the story of geologic time etched in the rock layers of the Grand Canyon? A knowledgeable interpreter opens the door to new dimensions of perception.

Involve the Visitor

Interpretive audiences are special. They come of their own free will ready to see their old world in fresh ways. They're on vacation; they're on their own time. They're not seeking lectures or schooling as much as inspiration and recreation. They want to be involved.

People at an interpretive program are not empty vessels passively waiting to be filled with environmental wisdom. They must associate new information with their past experiences. You must be aware, even in a general sense, of their backgrounds, interests, and experiences. You must appreciate how they see the environment in order to help them expand their perceptions of it.

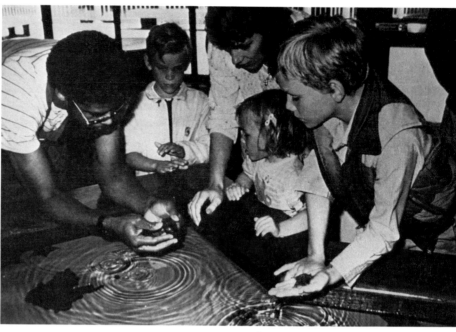

Courtesy of Monterey Bay Aquarium, California

Visitor curiosity is engaged through involvement in the touch tank at Monterey Bay Aquarium. Interpreters answer questions and help visitors learn about marine life.

Beggich-Boggs Visitor Center at Portage Glacier, Chugach Nat. Forest, AK, Courtesy of U.S.D.A. Forest Service

An interpreter helps visitors understand how Portage Glacier is formed and how it moves. Props and role playing make these difficult concepts understandable.

Interpreters walk a tightrope, balanced between two extremes. On one side are cold scientific facts. On the other is empty rhetoric filled with "ooh, ah" sentimentality. Good interpreters combine both ideas and emotions. They blend the extremes of taxonomy and tree hugging. Interpretive programs should involve the senses, challenge the intellect, and touch the emotions. They should entertain as well as inform.

Courtesy of Monterey Bay Aquarium

Developing Your Interpretive Style

It is natural to stand in awe of talented master interpreters who captivate audiences with their charisma and vast knowledge. There are no easy ways to become an outstanding interpreter. It requires dedication and desire. The raw materials include a love of people and a passion for your subject.

You can study the styles of successful interpreters and learn from their common attributes, but each one is unique. Their styles developed from their own personalities and life experiences.

Four interpreters that have served as models for many people are Josh Barkin, Dennis Olson, and Warren and Elizabeth Wells. They all learned to relate to their audiences in their own way.

Josh Barkin

The late Josh Barkin, San Francisco Bay Area naturalist, had a boundless enthusiasm that he shared with his audiences. A former businessman, Josh embraced his newfound profession with childlike wonder and he approached every new subject in a fresh way. Josh had a gift for using the simple, commonplace things to show people new worlds. *"A plant, a tree, a brook, a fern, a bird, a rock, and a lot of excitement and enthusiasm - you got a trip! What's all the baloney about the tremendous stuff you have to know? It adds on afterwards."*

The following is a typical Barkin field trip:

Courtesy of East Bay Regional Park District, Oakland, California

"A spider - there are so many different kinds of spiders it would drive you nuts! It's got eight legs - great. But a spider catches its prey and bites it...the venom is so slight it doesn't bother us, but it slows down the fly and then the spider drools and melts the tissue into a soup and then goes sl-u-r-p and the kids go y-u-k. They love gore, see, they love it! And you say, well, we use a straw don't we, to drink stuff. And, that's why you find flies in the web in the corner of the window all sort of desiccated or dried out because of the ability of the spider to do that, and if you were a spider you could demonstrate it. And you still don't know what kind of spider it is. I'm talking about story telling and adventure along the trail, and excitement. Alright, I'm a spider, OK? I have seven coils of rope, because he has seven spinnerets, this spider (he might have six, he might have five). I am carrying two buckets of glue and brushes. I take one coil of rope and throw it onto the tree and it sticks. Then I pull it tight and I run up as fast as I can so that the wind is whistling in my bronchi. Meanwhile I'm putting on the old stuff out of the glue bucket. I get there, and throw another line across horizontally, pull it in tight, and run like anything, at full speed. And that is the way a spider works. You've demonstrated something about a spider, you tell 'em. And then this very nice little lady who is along on the trip says, 'Oh, oh, look at the beautiful little hummingbird, isn't she sweet - the spider Y-U-K!' You say, 'Madame, if you love hummingbirds you have to be interested in spiders because no spiders, no hummingbird nests! The hummingbird ties his nest together with not only lichens and other materials, but with the spider thread - it is the tie that binds.' "

Using ropes and glue was commonplace for Josh. He was a great believer in props and gimmicks and loved to provoke his audience with them. A machete thrust in the ground (right) became an exciting tool for introducing people to vibrations, sounds, and the Old West.

Josh loved to keep his audiences a little off balance. What good is a tree? ... "Well, you can blow your nose in it!" His gutter walks changed trash in the streets into discarded artifacts of civilization. Josh helped people see their gray world through fresh eyes.

Ron Zimmerman

Dennis Olson

Dennis Olson, a Lake States naturalist, has developed an entire series of interpretive characters. His repertoire includes Critterman, Dr. Death, The Mad Herbalist, Gavin Immer - Professor of Loonacy, and Professor Avian Guano. Denny's characters are the vehicles for serious environmental messages. Each personality interacts with the audience, surprising and entertaining as they educate.

Professor Avian Guano enters the room. Long dark feathers protrude from his fingers. A yellow beak covers his nose. Bobbing his neck like an oversized chicken, he struts across the stage.

"Sooooo," he squeaks in a thick German accent, "you vant to learn about birds? I haf studied them so long I feel like dem." The professor goes on to interpret birds with slides, humorous anecdotes, outrageous props,

and some unwitting "volunteers." Members of the audience become contestants in a bird quiz show. The reward for a "wrong" answer is a huge shaving cream "bird dropping" on the head.

Denny's interpretation is filled with humor, drama, audience involvement, and physical props, but it is all based on solid natural history fact.

Olson says, "In my experience, kids and adults have remembered (word for word!) the major portions of Critterman, Mad Herbalist, and Dr. Guano shows. As interpreters, we have two obligations; we must give useful information and we must make it 'rememberable.' Theatrics internalizes concepts and information because the audience feels as well as learns.

Emotional or sensory experiences are remembered for a long time.

Good interpretive theatrics should make people apprehensive, happy, sad, and include the use of all five senses by the audience.

There is one hitch. It's a lot of work."

Photo courtesy of Dennis Olson

Warren and Elizabeth Wells

Warren Wells   Photos courtesy of Dave Imbrogno   Elizabeth Wells

There are many ways to prepare to become an interpretive naturalist. Warren Wells had been a professional trapper, hunter, fox farmer, prospector, daredevil motorcycle rider, tattoo artist, soldier, jeweler, lapidarist, and an employee of zoos and museums. A World War II veteran, he speaks Russian and Mandarin Chinese and served in the O.S.S. where he specialized in jungle and wilderness survival. He has unique experiences that he can relate to hundreds of natural scenarios.

Warren and Elizabeth Wells worked as an interpretive team for the Hamilton County Park District in Ohio for many years. Having "run together" at an early age, they developed a smooth working relationship.

Dave Imbrogno trained as an interpretive naturalist under the Wells. He later became Director of Programs for the Cincinnati Museum of Natural History. His thoughts on the Wells' style... *"The Wells' style"*

does more than teach, it inspires. Few people have casual contact with them. Most return again and again to learn more. Many go on to have natural history become a significant part of their lives. The Wells contact tens of thousands of people in their work as naturalists. Perhaps even more significantly they also inspire many to seek careers in the environmental field. I know, I am one. Offhand I can think of at least a dozen working professionals that I know of who got their start with the Wells. I am sure that there are many more. Warren and Elizabeth's contributions to the environment will increase geometrically with time as those who learned from them carry on the tradition. Their work will echo through generations."

Warren describes his style as that of a woodsman. Others have observed that he was a woodsman who loved people; someone who could make people feel good about themselves. He approaches every trail hike as if he were..."taking a bunch of

friends on a walk." A simple down home approach would draw in a high "fulutin" group as readily as a group of children. In a quiet relaxed voice that hinted of his South Carolinian roots, Warren might remark "Well that plant looks like it could be a mustard..." His understatement would often expand into a wealth of shared knowledge about this mystery plant that he actually knew well. "If it is a mustard, it'll have four petals that form a Maltese cross. That's why scientists call it the *Cruciferae* (the cross). The seeds develop all summer long. "Here, taste these." He'd talk about man's use of the mustard in England and maybe on American hotdogs. Meanwhile, Elizabeth would be "bird doggin'" for a new surprise down the trail. Two professionals, complementing each other's talents and learning something new each day. In Warren's words, "I never met a stranger and I never met anyone that I couldn't learn something from."

Finding Your Own Style

Experienced interpreters can be an inspiration to beginners. Much can be learned by watching them, but each of us must develop a style that we are comfortable with. Trying to duplicate the personality and background of a Josh Barkin would be insincere. The poise and ease of veterans like the Wells are pleasing to audiences, but it can't be imitated by a beginning naturalist. You can never be a Josh, Warren, Elizabeth, or Denny, but that should be a relief because then you are free to find your own style - to be yourself.

Chugach National Forest, Alaska

Donna Zimmerman

2
Planning Interpretive Experiences

I hear, I forget.
I see and hear, I remember.
I see, hear, and do, I understand.
- Old Chinese Proverb

Beggich-Boggs Visitor Center at Portage Glacier, Chugach National Forest, Alaska   Donna Zimmerman

The seasonal staff at the Beggich-Boggs Visitor Center prepares for the summer season. Themes relating to Portage Glacier and Portage Valley are important to visitors. With nearly one-half million people each summer, this is the most visited site in Alaska.

Choosing a Theme

Every successful interpretive presentation has a theme. The theme provides the plot for your story. It must be uppermost in your mind as you plan your presentation.

For example, you might be considering a talk on birds. "Birds" is too large a topic to cover in a single program. There are too many possibilities to give a unified program. You could narrow the theme to "peregrine falcons - the fastest predator in the world." Now your examples can be specific and striking. You can "paint pictures" of high speed dives. You can talk about the large feet that "club" other birds out of the air. You can show the group the notched beak that efficiently separates the vertebrae of the birds it stuns. You can tie ecological themes directly to the species: pesticides and thin egg shells, efforts to reintroduce them to skyscrapers "cliffs," and the need for conservation plans that don't stop at political boundaries.

Three Steps to Identifying Your Theme

1) **Select your topic (subject).**
   example: *Birds*

2) **Narrow your topic selection.**
   example: *Peregrine Falcons*

3) **Write your theme statement (specific message) as a complete sentence.**
   example: *Falcons are uniquely adapted to preying on other birds.*
   example: *Hunting with falcons has been the sport of nobility for centuries.*
   example: *Falcon populations have suffered world-wide decline due to the use of persistent pesticides.*

(more examples on pages 18-20)

Questions to ask when choosing a theme:

- **Is my theme stated as a complete sentence?** In the example above, a theme statement might read, "Falcons are uniquely adapted to preying on other birds." Keeping this one sentence in mind will help you to target your research.

- **Does my theme tell an important story about this site that will enrich the visitor's experience?** Why has this site been set aside? Does it have ecological or historical significance?

- **Is this a theme that my audience can relate to?** Highly technical information may not be appropriate for your audience? Would your visitors be interested in the adaptive radiation potential of *Carduelis tristis* (American goldfinch)? Better to give a program on attracting the "wild canary" to your backyard. Give specific examples that your audience can relate to: Goldfinches fly in an undulating pattern like a roller coaster. They sing their song on the wing, "potato chip, potato chip, ...potato chip..." They nest later than nearly all other songbirds as they wait for thistles to mature. They feed on the thistle seeds and line their nests with its down.

- **Is this a theme that I personally care about? Do I have the resources for research?** Freeman Tilden said it best, "Any interpretation presented without enthusiasm will be received without interest." You must care about the themes you select for your interpretive programs. Enthusiasm is contagious.

- **If a visitor were asked what my talk was about, would they be able to identify my theme?** If you can practice your talk in front of someone, ask them this question. If they can't tell you what your theme was, then run through this checklist again.

Researching Your Theme

Brainstorming has generated ideas. Now allow them to simmer until you can boil them down to a clear distillation of areas that can be researched.

Start at the library. As Josh Barkin once said, "I didn't learn these things in college. You dig it out of the library - Dewey Decimal System 500.1 to 599.6 - just sort of look through it."

Get to know your reference librarian. Use the "Reader's Guide to Periodical Literature," "ERIC," and other indexing systems. Read magazines, scientific journals, research reports, and nature literature.

Public agencies are rich sources of information. Conservation and natural resource departments, extension offices, and public health agencies produce numerous brochures on everything from managing a woodlot to life histories of resident wildlife.

You can ask local experts for local information. A wildlife manager at a nearby refuge can tell you when the tundra swans migrate through. A district soil conservationist can give you statistics on conservation practices in your county.

You can find historical information at your community historical society, museums, in the library archives, or from neighbors who make it

their hobby to study local history. Old newspapers stored on microfiche provide first person stories that give a real sense of the time.

There is no substitute for hard work if you want mastery of your subject. You won't use everything you learn through your research, but in-depth knowledge will give you the insight you need to develop your theme.

Doug Moore

Assessing Your Audience

The better you know your audience, the better you can prepare your program. What are their ages? Where are they from? What do they expect? Whatever their differences, all audiences share some universal likes and dislikes.

In a study of visitor perceptions of interpretive presentations at Northwest Trek, a wildlife park in Washington, Sam Ham found that visitors preferred the following (in order of importance):

Visitors like:
- Sensory involvement
- Humor
- New information made understandable
- An enthusiastic interpreter

Visitors do not like:
- Dry lectures
- An interpreter that talks too much
- A program that is too technical
- Long and unenthusiastic presentations

Finding Common Interests

Learn what you can about your audience and you'll soon find common strands of interest.

Relate to the experience of your audience. Comedians are adept at finding humor in common experiences. Knowing what visitors have in common - educational background, recreational experiences, cultural heroes - will help you choose better images for your message. For instance, comparing the underground tunnels of a prairie dog town to a city subway system would be more meaningful to an urban audience than a rural one.

A college ornithology class can relate to an olive-sided flycatcher when they learn that it wears a leisurely unbuttoned "vest" and calls "Quick! Three beers... Quick, three beers..."

You must involve your audience. People come to programs seeking a rewarding experience. Reward can be provided through physical, emotional, and intellectual involvement. That doesn't mean that you have to be a stand-up comedian or entertainer. What it means is that your message should be enlightening and that it should be entertaining.

Special Audiences

There is no "general" audience to which all interpretation applies. Each audience has unique characteristics and special needs. Some common special audiences are:
- children
- older adults
- foreign visitors
- minorities
- visually impaired
- hearing impaired
- ambulatory limited
- families

(Right) Courtesy of MN Valley National Wild. Refuge
Visitors who are unable to walk into the refuge participate in a program at the visitor center overlook.

Pictured Rocks National Lakeshore, Michigan   Warren Bielenberg
To succeed with family groups, involve the children.

Courtesy of Schmeeckle Reserve, Wisconsin
Be aware of the limitations of an older audience. On a woodcock walk, many elderly cannot hear the "peent" call of the woodcock without the aid of a parabolic recorder.

Needs of Special Audiences

Audience	Characteristics	Special Needs	Interpretive Requirements
Older Adults	Constitute 25-35% of our interpretive audiences in national parks. At retirement there is increased leisure time, diminished physical ability (mobility, hearing, sight), a vast experience base, less inhibition, and more sociability.	Appreciate opportunities to interact with others their age. Often returning visitors. Like in-depth and follow-up programs. Able to spend more time at park or center.	Avoid long or fast paced walks. Sight and hearing are often diminishing, so depth perception and listening activities can become a problem. Rely on vast experience of visitors and encourage interaction and sharing.
Foreign Visitors	Often with limited English skills, may lack experience or knowledge of resource being interpreted. Generally younger population, often well educated.	Be sensitive to the cultural etiquette of each nationality. Be cognizant of their language ability.	Avoid colloquial expressions. Speak slowly and deliberately. Take extra time to learn of their special interests. Never assume the "common" isn't worth pointing out.
Minorities	Many minority groups are frequently alienated from parks, natural areas, and historic sites which tend to over-represent majority traditions. Predominate ethnic minorities in U.S. are Native Americans, Afro-Americans, Hispanics, Chinese, Japanese.	Interpreter must assume responsibility for learning about each minority group and how their values and traditions are represented at each site.	Involve minorities in the interpretation of their own cultures or seek their input in developing programs.
Visually Impaired	Range from those whose vision has been corrected by glasses to those who "see" by hearing and touch.	Address these visitors directly, not through another person. Provide descriptions of objects, scenes, etc. Ask what help they care for if you are uncertain.	Involve via handling of objects.
Hearing Impaired	Almost 4% of our population suffers from hearing impairment. Generally, assume that older people will have some difficulty hearing.	Need to see the face of the interpreter. Need to see objects and be given visual outlines.	Keep hands away from mouth when speaking. Face visitor. Repeat important points and questions. Speak slowly.
Ambulatory Limited	Those who must use a wheelchair, crutches, leg braces, or walkers and canes in moving.	To be allowed equal access.	Limit walks to areas that are accessible. (Avoid steep slopes and rough terrain.)
Families	Wide range of motives for attending interpretive programs.	Lots of time to interact within the family unit. Learning is secondary to sharing time together.	Involving children will serve as a catalyst for whole family involvement.

Brainstorming

Brainstorming techniques can help you generate ideas that will develop your theme.

Whatever way you choose to brainstorm ideas, by yourself or with a group, find an environment that has no distractions. Record **all** ideas without judgment. Allow plenty of time to develop ideas. Even the most ridiculous thought might lead to a unique program theme. It should be a playful activity. Have fun with it.

Metaphor Session

A **metaphor session** is well suited for larger groups. During metaphor sessions, one person functions as the group facilitator while another person records the group's ideas on a large chalkboard or other visible surface.

To begin the session, write a key word on the board that relates to the topic. The group shouts out images, metaphors, and analogies as fast as they come to mind without judging any contributions. Each thought invites another. Each idea builds on the last. Sometimes two recorders are needed to keep up with the flow of ideas. After generating a full list of metaphors, have the group organize these ideas into related thoughts.

Synergic Comparison

Synergic comparison is another way to look at your topic. It means comparing unlike objects. You might generate a list like the following:

Beggich-Boggs Visitor Center at Portage Glacier, Chugach National Forest, Alaska   Donna Zimmerman
Brainstorming begins by finding a comfortable, distraction-free environment. One member records ideas without judgment.

"How is a snake like a tire?"
"How is a bird like an airplane?"
"How is an otter like a snowmobile?"
"How is a river like a person's circulatory system?"
"How is a tree like an apartment building?"
"How is goldenrod like McDonald's?

The less similar the objects - for example, if one is natural and one is man-made - the richer the comparison. Try to remove the cultural blinders with which we see everyday objects. How is a beaver like a typewriter? Play with this synergistic comparison and see what you get. Could you possibly get ideas for a talk on beavers?

How is a beaver like a typewriter?

- Both work with wood products.
- Both have rhythm.
- Both give a warning signal.
- Both have teeth.
- Both have four legs.
- Both make progress in small chunks.
- Both have "eyes."
- Both are capable of changing their environment.
- Both are very specialized.
- Both work "around" a wood product.
- Both see in black and white.
- Both require energy to work.
- Both "flood" their environment with their work - sometimes it's not wanted.
- Both work in pools.

Clustering

Clustering is one way to brainstorm on your own. Write a single theme in the center of a sheet of paper and circle it. Then jot down words and ideas as fast as they come to mind. Key concepts and patterns will automatically create a framework for your program.

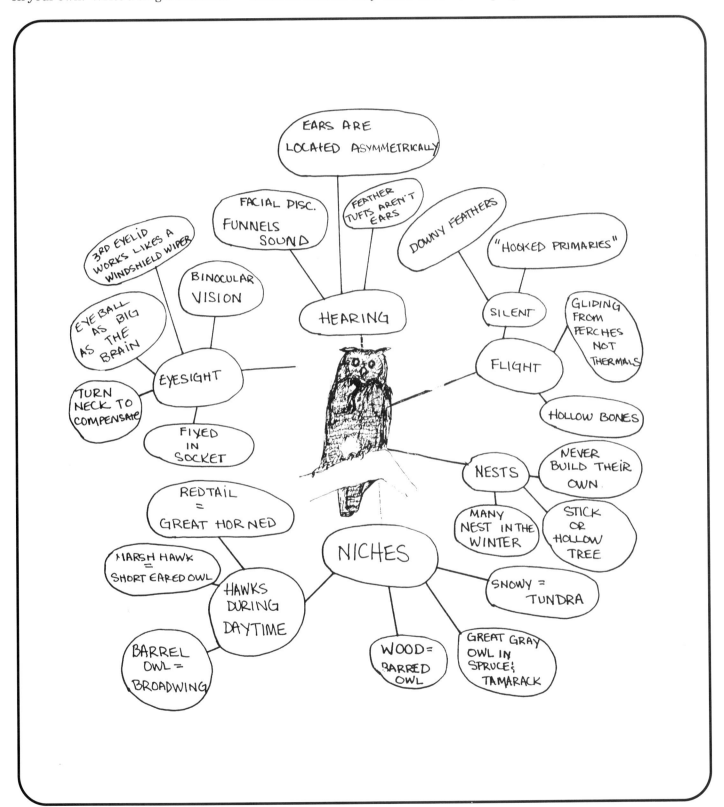

Steps in Planning an Interpretive Program

Example #1
Point Iroquois
Lighthouse Tour

Point Iroquois Lighthouse, Hiawatha National Forest, Michigan

Michael Gross

Select a topic	Point Iroquois Lighthouse Tour
Narrow topic to one main idea/theme	Lighthouse was a home.
Write a theme statement as a single sentence	"The Point Iroquois lighthouse was home for three keepers and their families."

Research the theme	Research Sources:
	    Brimley-Bay Mills Historical Society
	    Iroquois Point lightkeepers' logs
	    Interviews with families who lived at Point Iroquois
	    Books about lighthouses from Sault St. Marie library
	    Great Lakes Lighthouse Association
	    U.S. Coast Guard, Sault St. Marie Office
	    Interpretive Master Plan for lighthouse

Identify the audience	Have interviews with interpretive staff. Check for potential visitors with local Chamber of Commerce office. Observe and interview visitors.
Brainstorm interpretive options	Use a photographic scrapbook of families who lived in the lighthouse as an interpretive prop. Tell stories of the tragedies and joys of the people who lived here (i.e., twins Floyd and Loyd Bredlow born in an upstairs bedroom August, 1913; died in November, 1913).

(continued)

	Explain the purpose of each room and building and tell some interesting stories about them (i.e., oilhouse where kerosene for the light was stored safely away from lightning strikes at the tower). Tell stories and show pictures of the keepers children attending school with their very own schoolteacher. Show objects like: Toy top found on site by restoration team. The old oven where cinnamon rolls were baked during the late night watches. The stacks of wood that were prepared by the children to keep the stone and brick lighthouse warm. A photographic scrapbook of families who lived in the lighthouse as an interpretive prop.
Develop interpretive presentation	See the options and the steps in developing a presentation in Chapters 3-7.

Example #2 "Songs of the Wetlands" Talk

Songs of the Wetlands

Share an evening walk to hear the springtime symphony of frogs. Learn to identify individual calls.

Thursday, May 3, 8:30 - 9:15 p.m.
Schmeeckle Reserve Visitor Center

Select a topic	Frogs in the Schmeeckle Reserve
Narrow topic to one main idea/theme	To encourage people to enjoy the early spring courtship of frogs in the Schmeeckle Reserve wetlands.
Write theme statement as a single sentence	"As water temperatures rise, three species of frogs emerge from their winter hibernation in Schmeeckle Reserve wetlands to engage in a spirited courtship."

(continued)

Research the theme	Research Sources:
	  First-hand experience in the wetlands
	  Reptiles and Amphibians of Wisconsin by Vogt
	  Seasonal records and census data from Schmeeckle
	    Reserve files and Professor Ray Anderson's research
	  Tape recording of Wisconsin frogs from UWSP Student Chapter of The Wildlife Society
	  Articles from magazines like Audubon, National
	    Wildlife, Wisconsin Natural Resources Magazine
	  Nature essays such as Hal Borland, Loren Eisley,
	    etc.

Identify the audience	Look at past participation in Schmeeckle Reserve programs (records and other staff). Target promotion to attract family groups (flyers in library, community events in local newspaper).
Brainstorm interpretive options	Hand-out noise makers to simulate calls of various frogs. Have aquariums with captured live frogs. Use slides and taped frog sounds. Have charts illustrating breeding season and the relationship to water temperature. Have various containers of water at temperature each species begins calling. Discuss the importance of frogs as indicators of a healthy ecosystem.
Develop interpretive presentation	See the options and the steps in developing a presentation in Chapters 3-7.

3
Interpretive Talks

Let thy speech be better than silence,
or be silent.
- Dionysus the Elder

Chugach National Forest, Alaska

Courtesy of U.S.D.A. Forest Service

A campfire program in the Willawaw campground explores the theme "Wolves: vital or vicious?"

Talks are the fundamental tool of interpreters. Interpreters give talks in visitor centers, at campfires, or at major features, like Old Faithful. Talks are also given off-site at schools, service club meetings, and on radio or television.

Talks may take many forms. Interpreters give orientation programs, do demonstrations, present audio-visual programs, use props, do characterizations, and are story tellers. Any successful talk has two key elements: structure and substance.

Structuring Your Talk

Audiences cringe at decapitated chicken presentations, talks that flop around in all directions with no conscious purpose. Audiences want talks that stand up and crow. They want to be awakened by your first words. They want to be marched off as a flock to feed on a meaningful flow of ideas.

There are many ways to create a flow of ideas, but here is a simple four step strategy.

Step 1: Pow. Capture the group's attention with a provocative introduction.

Step 2: Bridge. Answer the questions, "Why was that said?" and "What does it mean to me?"

Step 3: Body. Illustrate the main message of your program with examples. Listeners enjoy personalized "for instances."

Step 4: Conclusion. Conclude your presentation by summarizing or giving a call to action. Answer the question "So what?"

Pow

An introduction does two things. It promises your listeners a rewarding experience and it introduces your talk theme.

Your introduction can be startling or humorous, a rhetorical question or an apt quotation. Your goal is provocation. You need to grab your audience with your first words.

For instance, when a county naturalist spoke to a local hunters club about their image, he ignited interest with: "Hunters are bloodthirsty slobs trying to prove their masculinity." He quickly added, "That's what I read in an animal rights newsletter today."

An introduction doesn't need to be a verbal firebomb to be provocative. One plant lore program began when a hooded monk, illuminated by a flaming mullein stalk, stepped into the darkened room. "With this

'witch's candle,' I'll take you back to the time when plants symbolized our gods and demons and healed our bodies."

Aside from catching a group's attention, the pow introduces the program's theme and sets group expectations.

Chugach National Forest, Alaska
Courtesy of U.S.D.A. Forest Service
"Smokey" helps the interpreter with a bear safety talk. His entrance was an effective "pow" for a Willawaw campfire talk.

Bridge

Bridges connect the introduction to the body of the talk and to the interests of the audience. For example, in the talk to the hunter group, the interpreter began to build a bridge when he said, "That's what I read in an animal rights newsletter today. We have an image problem. Hunters will lose their sport if we don't collectively work toward changing our image."

Bridges should answer the questions, "OK, you have my attention, but what's your purpose? Why should I care?"

Body

Your theme serves as the skeleton to which you attach your ideas. The body is made up of facts and for instances that flesh out your theme. Without a theme, the body of your talk will be flabby and shapeless with little appeal to your audience.

Limit the number of ideas presented in the body. Psychological researcher G. A. Miller theorizes that people best understand and remember new information when it is "chunked" into seven categories or less.

With your main points outlined, you now must decide how to illustrate them. To be effective, every major idea presented should be illustrated in some way. Use visual aids, such as props, slides, or other audio visual devices. Create mental images through metaphor and analogy, guided imagery, or story telling. Involve the audience physically. Make sure you breathe life into cold dead abstractions.

"To be effective, every major idea presented should be illustrated in some way."

Beggich-Boggs Visitor Center at Portage Glacier, Chugach National Forest, Alaska   U.S.D.A. Forest Service
An interpreter uses imagery (above) and visual aids (below) to interpret glacier formation.

Conclusion

Your conclusion should tell the listener you are done. It can be a call to action or can summarize your main points. It might be a thought provoking quote or a dramatic ending for emotional impact.

U.S.D.A. Forest Service

One interpreter created a dramatic mood at a campfire talk by speaking from behind a lighted candle. She talked about fears of the night and eased them by telling stories of animals that live in the night. She ended her talk by blowing out the candle and inviting the audience on a night walk.

How to Give a Talk

Setting the Stage

You begin "speaking" to your audience long before you utter your first words. Your grooming whispers about your dependability. Your posture states your competence. Your clothing shouts your credibility as an expert on the subject.

Be appropriately groomed and dressed with an alert, confident posture. Let your appearance assure the audience that you are competent. Don't let them wonder if you are.

Be a good host. Arrive before your audience in time to ready equipment, prepare props, and check that everything is set for your guests.

By the time the first visitors arrive you should be ready to make as many acquaintances as possible. Your warmth can melt barriers that exist between strangers. Gather some insights about your audience during your talk. One naturalist discovered he had a doctor from a poison center at his edible wild foods talk. This doctor was a great addition to the program when poisonous plants were shown.

Many members of the audience may have something to show or something that you can relate to. A rancher has unique perspectives on prairies. A language teacher has a particular interest in the root meanings of plant names.

Come prepared. You should know your subject so well that you can concentrate on your delivery and respond to your audience.

Bryd Visitor Center, Shenandoah National Park, Virginia   Warren Bielenberg
Well groomed, friendly and confident, an interpreter presents the "bear facts."

Your Beginning

The first thirty seconds of your talk are critical in establishing rapport. You need to project warmth, confidence, and competence. To do this, you must feel prepared. You should have practiced your talk so that it flows easily.

Don't put barriers between you and your audience. Don't stand behind a podium or a table. Meet the audience standing upright with a smile and eye to eye contact. Be casual but not sloppy. Don't sit down or stand with hands in your pockets. Don't be too formal though, with hands behind you, wooden posture, and gloomy expression.

Monterey Bay Aquarium, CA   Ron Zimmerman
Divers give a talk on marine life at Monterey Bay Aquarium.

Notes

Don't write out your talk. Notes can become a crutch and impede your eye contact and gestures. At most, have an outline on a notecard. If you need a cue to get back on track, simply pause, look at your notecard, and carry on. Make this act seem natural. Don't hide your notecards or it will look like you are "sneaking a peek," and it will disrupt the flow of the talk.

Don't memorize your talks. It will prevent a fresh spontaneous delivery. Instead, picture your talk from start to finish. Keep the main points in mind and you will easily remember the examples that illustrate them.

Voice

Talk with the same conversational inflections that you would use with a group of friends. You are not delivering a scientific paper. Speak spontaneously and with simple directness.

Your voice is an instrument. Learn to play it. Beethoven's Moonlight Sonata arrests us with variations in pitch, volume, and rate. The unceasing monotony of Muzak, on the other hand, serves only as dull background. Play Beethoven, not Muzak.

Orchestrate your talk with a contrast of high and low notes. Use the full range of your voice. Emphasize some parts of your talk with a slow, deliberate pace. Breeze through other parts lightly.

Moments of silence can be used to set off main points of your talk. Pauses are like speed bumps on a road; they alert your audience that something important is coming up.

Little Bighorn Battlefield National Monument, Montana   Michael Gross

An interpreter in cavalry uniform demonstrates the equipment of a frontier soldier. (below) A Native American recreates "The Battle of Greasy Grass" by evoking images and emotions through gestures, phrases, and tone of voice.

Little Bighorn Battlefield National Monument, MT
Michael Gross

The Words You Use

Well chosen words create vivid images. The time you spend in choosing words will be appreciated by your audience.

Be specific. The statement, "People often shoot porcupines because they damage trees." conveys a vague image. Compare that to "I know a woodsman from Polonia, who blasts a dozen porcupines a year for stripping bark off his white pines."

Why does the second statement convey a sharper image? It refers to a specific person (even better if you could name him) in a specific place with porcupines in specific trees. He doesn't just shoot porcupines, he blasts them. The personal pronoun "I" tells us this is a real story you can vouch for.

For more effective imagery, **use active verbs, specific, concrete nouns, familiar people and places, and personal language.**

Avoid Fillers. Avoid unnecessary words. Trite expressions, cliches, redundancies, ahs and ums, and "weasel words" are fillers. Those trained in science are particularly adept at using "weasel words," or disclaimers like, "According to Jones," or "It would appear that..." Eliminate fillers from your talk.

Body Language

We communicate with our arms, face, and posture. As Sigmund Freud said, "No mortal can keep a secret. If his lips are silent, he talks with his fingertips, betrayal oozes out of him at every pore."

Jim Hardin

All animals communicate through body movements. Canines, for example, reveal messages through posture, facial expressions and tail positions.

Communicate through facial expressions. Some experts claim that fifty-five percent of understanding from messages is from facial expressions, not words.

In our culture, eyes are especially important. Look at your audience all the time. Make friendly eye contact with everyone.

Communicate through posture. Alert posture conveys confidence. Use body language to punctuate ideas.

Avoid distracting mannerisms. Are you nervous about giving a talk? You aren't alone. Actor Sir Lawrence Olivier got physically ill before every performance. A good performer like Olivier nets those butterflies and puts them to use. Convert nervousness to energy. But, don't let nervousness spill out into distracting mannerisms. Guard against:

- weight shifting
- body rocking
- table leaning
- arm swinging
- hand hiding
- clothes fidgeting
- foot scuffling

Warren County Cons. Area, Iowa   Paul Regnier

Body language is as important as your voice.

Communicate through gestures. Punctuate and describe points in the program with your hands. Use natural, unexaggerated gestures. Be tasteful and understated. Good gestures do not call attention to themselves. They fit the content of the message and reinforce ideas.

Walk with purpose. Ducks waddle, ostriches strut, elephants trudge, and panthers stalk. The way you walk conveys your image. Choreograph your performance. Every movement should have purpose; it should either draw the audience's attention or punctuate an important point.

Walking toward listeners focuses their attention on the next thing you say. Timing is critical. Your movement should start just before you make your statements.

Fluid movement takes practice. Rehearse your movements as thoroughly as you do your talk.

Aboriginal petroglyphs, Ku-Ring-Gai Chase National Park, New South Wales, Australia   Donna Zimmerman

An interpreter describes an emu etched in the rocks. Descriptive body language can communicate enthusiasm and paint mental images.

Props

People pay attention to things they are curious about. Props heighten curiosity, especially when they are used provocatively.

Mounted specimens are effective props. A redheaded woodpecker mount can tell an audience a lot about cavity dwellers. People can see the special arrangement of toes and can feel the tail feathers.

Props can give you credibility. Tools like a spotting scope or a parabolic recorder create an aura of expertise. Holding a ten-gauge shotgun while telling the story of the passenger pigeon adds authenticity to your tale. Quoting Thoreau from a frayed, yellow copy of *Walden Pond* helps create atmosphere.

Tips for Using Props

- **People respond to familiar objects when they are used in innovative ways.** Such props help you draw analogies between common objects and the natural world. Assembling a flashlight - batteries and all - clearly shows the concept of interdependence, the idea that different parts work together to make a system.

- **Colors draw attention.** Red excites people. Green and blue reduce tension. Colors can have cultural significance as well. Who do you think of when you see ruby red shoes? A pig-tailed girl from Kansas and her scruffy dog Toto. Why not use this prop to metaphorically lead a group down the yellow brick road?

- **Involve different senses with props.** Odors and noises capture a group's attention. For example, owl calls can draw in people as well as owls. Reveal that great horned owls prey on skunks by opening a jar of skunk scent (but quickly!).

- **Involve people with props.** A visitor who touches the soft plumage of an owl will appreciate its silent flight. If they hold an owl egg, they'll never forget its shape or color. We remember what we experience.

- **People are drawn to historical artifacts.** Artifacts create an atmosphere of a bygone era. Rolling a big log with an old cant hook or touching the button from the jacket of a Confederate soldier are ways of traveling through time.

Yellowstone National Park, Wyoming

Alan Leftridge

Bears are a "must tell" story in Yellowstone National Park. A skull becomes a physical connection between visitors and wild bears. Handling the skull is a memorable experience. Words and facts alone are not as effective in making the connections.

Cultural Demonstrations

Props and visitor participation are key elements in a cultural demonstration. Period costumes can lend authenticity.

George Rogers Clark National Monument, Indiana   Warren Bielenberg
A "redcoat" uniform is the focus of a demonstration.

Warren Bielenberg

Shenandoah National Park, Virginia   Warren Bielenberg
Old musical toys are demonstrated in a "folkways" talk. Visitors are invited to "try it."

Indiana Dunes National Lakeshore, Indiana   Warren Bielenberg

Spring thaws, hotcakes, and sweet things make maple syruping demonstrations popular.

Delaware Water Gap N.R.A., NJ,Warren Bielenberg

The self-sufficient ingenuity of past generations fascinate us.

Chugach National Forest, Alaska   Courtesy of U.S.D.A. Forest Service

Denali National Park, Alaska   Donna Zimmerman

Isle Royale National Park, Michigan   Warren Bielenberg

(Above left) The lure of gold still draws modern day prospectors to a program.

(Above right) Sleds and dogs, used for winter patrols at Denali, intrigue visitors from gentler climates.

(Left) A commercial fishing program involves the senses while showing how herring are smoked.

Humor

One naturalist began an evening talk on calling barred owls with a story from his own experience:

There's a danger in coming too close to another species. The danger could be that you'll be misunderstood by that species. Or, more often, that your actions will be misinterpreted by your own species. My personal experiences have often involved the latter.

I house a barred owl in my basement. It happens he has only one eye. I call him Jerry. We often visit school groups which requires he be transported in a portable dog kennel.

Jerry   Donna Zimmerman

Being of an independent nature, Jerry sometimes enters or leaves the kennel with reluctance. Such was the occasion several weeks ago.

After some near misses at capturing him, I found myself leaning into the dog kennel on hands and knees. Jerry jumped on my back. After some careful consideration, I determined that the most expedient and logical maneuver would be to simply crawl to his flight cage on the other side of the basement.

As we concentrated on getting around piles of sorted laundry, I suddenly realized that I was being watched. My twelve year old son had brought home a friend--his first visit.Their four eyes were glued on us. Our three eyes stared back... It was at this point that I realized there were social dangers in getting too close to owls.

Let me share with you some other close encounters with owls. I have brought slides...

Tips for Using Humor

The story above illustrates several points about use of humor.

• The humorous story relates to the talk theme. It makes a point about the subject. Even if no one laughed aloud, it serves as an appropriate introduction to the evening's talk. **Humor should only be used if it illustrates an important point.** If it is used only to gain a laugh, it is inappropriate.

• Use a story if it is inoffensive and is one with which the audience can identify. Commonplace incidents can take on humorous aspects when seen from a new perspective. It is important to exercise good taste and not embarrass your audience. If anyone is a target of the humor, make it you.

• A humorous story or anecdote should arrive unannounced. It should drift in and out of the plot as unobtrusively as Clark Kent, not as flamboyantly as Superman.

• Humor requires timing and delivery to be effective. Use it only if you feel comfortable with it and understand it.

Questioning

Many interpreters question visitors to get them involved. Questioning is a highly useful skill to add to your repertoire.

Questions serve several purposes:

- They stimulate interest.
- They help organize a program.
- They encourage creative thinking.
- They emphasize important points.
- They offer visitors a chance to share thoughts and feelings.

Jefferson National Expansion Memorial, St. Louis, Missouri   N.G. Messinger

Purposeful questions create a dialog. New levels of understanding result from this strategy.

Types of Questions

Ask different types of questions during a program. Let each question have a preconceived purpose, however. Quality not quantity of questions is the key to a good presentation.

- **Focus questions,** the most basic kind of questions, ask for specific information. They often begin with "who, what, or where." For example:

"What have you heard about acid rain?"
"What do you observe about the cricket chorus we hear?"
"What does this snake feel like?"
"What do you observe about this barred owl that makes it a perfect night hunter?"
"Where are the white pines distributed in the forest, compared to the cedars?"

Focus questions help to structure a program and solicit involvement. However, they do not always provoke creative thinking.

- **Process questions** have a wider scope of possible responses than focus questions. Process questions ask people to integrate information rather than just re-membering or describing.

Process questions often begin with "What does this mean? What would happen if...? What experience supports...? Why did...?" For example:
"What evidence indicates acid rain is affecting this lake?"
"Why do crickets chirp?"
"How does a snake keep its cool?"
"Why do owls have disks around their eyes/face?"
"Why are there more of these cedars down here and more of those white pines up there?"

- **Evaluative questions** usually deal with matters of value, choice or judgment of the participants. They offer group members a chance to express their feelings. Evaluative questions often begin with "What do you think? What about..." For example:
"What do you think should be done about acid rain?"
"How could crickets communicate if they couldn't chirp?"
"Why do people think snakes are slimy, repulsive creatures?"
"How would owls have to change if all of their prey were active during the day?"
"Why is it important to have different kinds of trees in a forest?"

Rhetorical Questions

Not all questions require a verbal response from visitors. **Rhetorical questions** are asked when you don't expect visitors to answer aloud.

Involving and dramatic, rhetorical questions help emphasize important points in a program. For example, "If we do not solve air pollution, what will become of our Northeastern forests? What will become of the pine and oak we depend on for our houses? What will we do when there are no more maple trees and no more maple syrup for our pancakes? What will happen to the plants and animals that depend on those trees for food, shelter, and protection?" These questions don't demand a response, but they do involve the listener.

Tips for Questioning

- Direct most questions to the entire audience rather than a single individual. This indicates to the group that everyone is expected to think.

- Ask only one question at a time.

- Allow time for an answer. This is called "wait-time." Research has shown the longer the questioner allows for an answer, the better the answer will be. Never answer your own questions. If no one offers a response, leave it open to be answered later or rephrase the question.

- Do not start a question with "Does anyone know..." or "Can anyone tell me..." Such phrases express doubt that the question can be answered.

- Pace questions to the ability of the group.

- Develop ideas and concepts through a series of questions. Build from focus questions to process questions to evaluative questions. This challenges your group to higher levels of thinking.

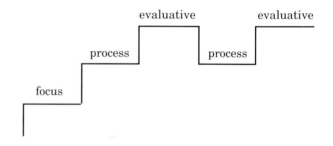

- Accept answers to questions gracefully, even if the answers are wrong. Never make someone feel foolish for participating in the program.

- Finally, never ask a question that requires a simple yes or no.

4
Slide Talks

Text and photographs (unless otherwise noted) by Douglas L. Moore, Media Specialist in Natural Resources, University Graphics & Photography, University of Wisconsin - Stevens Point.

Slides have long served as a useful medium for interpreters. Interpreters give slide talks in campfire bowls, visitor centers, and off-site at service club meetings and community halls.

Thirty-five millimeter slides are an "old" technology dating to the 1930's. With new cameras, projectors and computer-assisted technologies, the slide talk has become an even more effective way to share ideas and tell stories about interpretive sites.

Advantages of Slides

- In a darkened room, they command every moment of the viewer's attention.

- Slide images enhance the spoken word and can sometimes relate the message without narration.

- Slides provide sharp, vividly colored images. They can be used with any size audience or meeting room.

- Programs can be easily changed, edited, or reshuffled.

- Sound, simulated motion, and other special effects can be incorporated into a slide show.

- Slide shows can be transferred to video, rarely vice-versa.

- Equipment needed to produce and project images is modestly priced and simple to operate.

- Presenters who use slides project a credible, professional image.

Creating Slide Talks

Think of a good movie you've seen recently. How did it begin? What was the plot? How did the storyline develop? What scenes and transitions told the story? How did it end?

You should strive to tell a story with slides. Every good slide talk has a beginning, middle and an end (or pow, bridge, body, conclusion) as described in Chapter 2. Every good slide talk has a plot (theme), and unified sequences of images and narration to develop that theme.

Where do you start? Resist the temptation to grab pencil and paper and start outlining your talk. The logical process of outlining will usually result in a colorless, unexciting script. Good slide talks are the result of several creative steps.

Steps in Creating a Slide Talk

- Select a topic that is best interpreted by slides (e.g. wildlife that is seldom seen, dynamic changes on the landscape or stories from the past).

- Narrow your topic and identify the theme (see Chapter Two for processes in theme development).

- Research your topic until you are thoroughly familiar with it. Identify the audience (see Chapter Two).

- Imagine the story as a flow of images.

- Free-write a rough script from these mental images.

- Edit the script into a note-card storyboard.

- Select slides and special effects that illustrate the story. Edit images on a light table for visual flow and impact.

- Transfer slides to a tray. Practice thoroughly.

Imaging a script.

Free-writing.

Imaging a Slide Talk

Imaging a script allows you to integrate visual images, sensory impressions and feelings into your talk. It is a simple and fun process. Just lean back and daydream through your slide story. Visualize the pictures, see the sequences unfold, experience the close-ups as well as the grand vistas, listen to the sounds and smell the fragrances.

Free-Writing

Open your eyes and put it on paper. Write it out just as you saw it in your imagination. Jot down thoughts, feelings, sights, sounds and smells you imagined. Let the ideas flow unedited onto the paper.

The Storyboard

Once the full richness of your slide story is imagined, you can begin to arrange the slide talk into a storyboard.

Notecards are ideal for use in a storyboard. Simply sketch or describe the image to be illustrated, and write out the narration that goes with it. Later, the notecards can be used as you practice the talk, and they can easily be changed as ideas and images are added or subtracted.

(Above and left) Editing the rough script into a notecard storyboard.

Editing the Storyboard

- Stick to your theme and limit the scope of your talk. Don't try to present everything known on the subject.

- Strive for a concise, exciting program. Thirty minutes may be ideal for an auditorium program. Seldom exceed 45 minutes. Orientation slide programs for people touring your site must be much shorter, perhaps 5-15 minutes.

- Organize and develop sequences of slides that develop a single idea.

- Plan transitions between sequences that link them together.

- Use visually exciting, fast-paced sequences at the beginning and end. Start with a pow, build to a climax.

- Edit for visual flow. For example, start with a wide view for orientation and zoom to a close-up. Compare and contrast environmental conditions, before and after, cause and effect.

- Resist the urge to project redundant images, for example, showing three sunset slides when one will have more impact.

- Use sounds to create unity. A quiet "ticking of a geologic clock" can accompany photos of glaciers, then change to the rhythmic chopping of an axe in the hand of early man.

- Limit narration to about 15 seconds per slide. Keep the images moving, but vary the pace.

Example of a Visual Sequence

This opening sequence gives a historical perspective to a nature reserve. The sequence opens with the ticking of a clock as we view a pristine forest. This sound is replaced by the chopping of axes and pictures of loggers. A stump provides the visual transition to the present-day story.

1

2

3

4

5

6

7

8

Illustrating a Slide Talk

Ideally, you should select or create slides only after the storyboard is completed. Practically, however, the storyboard is often created with available slides in mind. In fact, you may find it helpful to develop your storyboard as you sort slides on a light table.

There are four ways to obtain slides:
• Select from your slide files.
• Shoot camera originals.
• Purchase them from photographers and distributors.
• Make copy from magazines and other printed material.

The last option should be used only if you have received permission of the publisher and photographer, or if you are using it for one-time non-profit educational purposes. (Fair use doctrine of federal copyright laws)

A big light table is indispensable for assembling, sorting, and culling images. You can make an industrial-sized one quite cheaply by placing a sheet of translucent white acrylic over an inverted 2' x 4' fluorescent fixture.

Creating and Composing Images

A photograph may be technically excellent (sharp and well-exposed), yet lack the elusive quality of "impact." To enhance the power of visual communication, consider the guidelines on the following pages when you take photographs and design speaker support slides.

Get Close

Make the subject obvious. Don't make the viewer guess the intent of the photograph. Before you press the shutter, you should be able to ver-bally define what the image is meant to convey. The best way to emphasize the subject: get close. Eliminate dis-tracting foreground and background and focus on the subject. Lead in to the subject from the corner. Lighting also draws attention to the subject.

Create a Dynamic Balance

Informal balance, employing an odd number of elements, off-center, is seen as dynamic, and holds viewer atten-tion longer. Formal balance is sym-metrical and static. Informal balance is often expressed in the "rule of thirds." As you photograph, imagine the frame divided like a tic-tac-toe board. Place the subject at one of the four intersections.

Format

Use vertical slides where appropriate. Tall subjects are often best photographed vertically. Vertical suggests a dynamic posture, whereas horizontal is the angle of repose. However, vertical slides present problems with small screens, low ceilings, and dissolve shows. Photograph important subjects both vertically and horizontally.

Color

Color has emotional impact. Warm colors appear to advance, while cool colors recede. Color can contribute emphasis and separate elements. Consider the visual impact of a warm, bright subject juxtaposed against a cool, darker background.

Depth

Use images that give the impression of three-dimensions. Many slide photos, particularly landscapes and other wide views, appear "flat" and far away. You can lend depth to photographs by including something prominent in the foreground, by using side-lighting, or by framing the scene, which creates a window effect.

Speaker Support (Title/Graphic) Slides

A title, graph, chart, drawing, map, or diagram may help to illustrate a point, lend organization, and polish your presentation. Make these visuals simple and brief.

This map of the Voyageur's route was simplified in the slide at right.

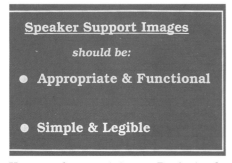

Keep words to a minimum. Don't simply transfer whole sentences and paragraphs from the printed page. Use symbols or bullets and paraphrase sentences.

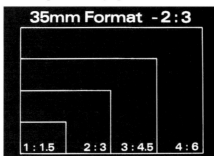

For maximum size and legibility, title/graphic slides should be designed to fit a 2:3 format.

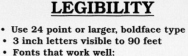

Employ simple fonts and big, bold lettering.

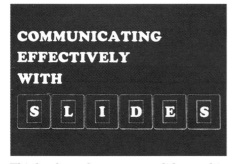

Think of speaker support slides as big billboards or posters. Limit text to 25 words or less. Legibility is influenced by background contrast.

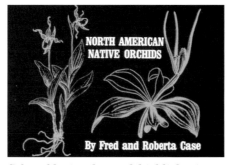

Color adds visual appeal, highlights important points and separates elements. Since the eye is drawn toward the brightest areas, "reverse-text" slides are often used, with bright titles or drawings on a darker background. These can be created with films like Kodalith® or Vericolor Slide Film®.

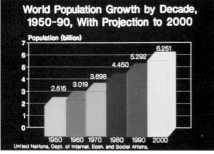

With a color monitor, appropriate software, and access to a film recorder, you can create professional-looking graphics on the screen and transfer them to 35mm color slide film.

"Burn-on" or "sandwich" slides combine a picture background with graphics for a visual "double-whammy." A slide duplicator is used to meld the two images together. (Photo by Robert Korth)

With slide presentations, less is better than more. Don't use more visuals, especially title/graphic slides, than you need to get the message across. Visual aids (including slides) are meant to enhance and supplement the live narration, not supplant it.

Slide Showmanship

You, the interpreter, are more important than the pictures on the screen. They serve only to illustrate your thoughts, ideas and feelings. You provide the warmth, humor and rapport.

A good slide show is an interplay between audience and interpreter. It requires that the interpreter respond to the moods, interests and reactions of the audience.

Your presentation should be so well rehearsed that you don't have to think about what you are going to say, but rather, how you say it as you relate to your audience. Rehearse by reviewing your storyboard cards. When you have the images and narration in your mind, present the show to an audience (friends or relatives) and ask for critical feedback.

Presentation Techniques

- Face the audience from the front of the room. Don't turn your back on them to look at slides as you talk.

- Do not refer to each slide as it appears on the screen. Let the slide illustrate what you are talking about. For example, do not say, "This is a tree."

- Use voice inflections to keep the narration interesting. Gestures are ineffective in a darkened room.

- Verbally anticipate the next slide. Don't wait for it to appear as a cue before you advance to your next point.

- Under most circumstances, display a slide on the screen no longer than 10-15 seconds. The audience will begin to study it and stop listening to your point. Flaws in a photo begin to "materialize" after about 15 seconds.

- Never apologize for your slides or your program. It will make your audience uncomfortable and you will lose credibility.

- Pay attention to tempo when changing slides. Change the rhythm to suit the storyline and action sequences.

- Never allow an empty white screen to "blind" your audience.

- Calmly resolve breakdowns: if a projector bulb blows, turn on the room lights, and quickly replace it. If a slide gets stuck and the projector won't advance, use a coin to remove the tray, then dislodge the offending slide. Reset the tray and resume the program where you left off.

- Arrange to have someone operate the room lights and adjust projector focus while you remain in front of the group.

Special Effects

Slides are a versatile medium. Additional equipment and preparation time, can help you embellish your presentation with special effects:

- dissolve using two or more projectors
- two or more screens, and/or a panorama effect
- music and sound effects

Creating special effects is expensive and time consuming. Poorly done, they detract from a presentation. Take time to prepare.

Music and sound effects are copied onto a tape for use in a live presentation. Use of copyrighted music requires permission and possibly "needle-drop" fees. Copyright-free music and sound effects can be purchased or, with a local musician and live sounds, you can record your own.

A two-projector dissolve set-up.

Dissolve sequences can simulate motion.

Photos by Michael Gross

A dissolve unit fades images from one to another, making viewing much easier on the audience. With such a device, you can create special effects, show more slides and give your presentation a more polished and professional luster. On the other hand, with the required two (or more) projectors, extra tray(s), a power strip, and more cords and connections, the mechanical and logistical preparations for a dissolve show are more involved.

Many modern dissolve units offer other features for special effects. Desirable options include:

- several dissolve rates, from "cut" to 8 seconds
- built-in memory - allows you to create, store, and retrieve complex dissolve sequences
- remote operation

Equipment

Room/Equipment Checklist

Before the first member of your audience sits down, you should check the following:

- Can the meeting room be sufficiently darkened?

- Will the entire audience have a clear view of the screen?

- Is the screen large enough for the size of the audience?

- Are grounded electrical outlets handy? Will extension cords be needed?

- Are projection stand height and size sufficient?

- Have you tested the projector, and are spare bulbs available?

- Are audio equipment and dissolve unit functioning? (if applicable)

- Do slides project and drop properly? Are there lock rings on projector trays?

- Are remote control cord(s) long enough and do they work properly? (Check slide reverse, forward, remote focus and autofocus.)

- Have you previewed your program to eliminate upside down and backward slides?

- Is the projector level, and image size adjusted to fit the screen?

- Will room acoustics allow your voice to be heard from the back, even with projector noise?

- Will you need a lighted lectern or pointer?

- Are cords taped to the floor with duct tape?

- Have you arranged to have room lights dimmed down or turned off?

Choosing a Slide Projector

Kodak Carousel® and Ektagraphic® projectors and their clones are the overwhelming choice for 35mm slide presentations. The Ektagraphic® models, designed for professional/institutional A-V use, are a bit more rugged. All Kodak projectors feature easy-access bulb changing, reading light, remote control outlet, and convenient leveling feet. Other features available: remote focus, autofocus, timer, lighted control panel, preview screen. **Use a zoom lens**. It allows you to size the image to the screen without moving the projector.

Projector trays hold 80 or 140 slides. Use only plastic-mounted slides in larger capacity trays; they won't become dog-eared as paper mounts do, which often jam.

5
Creative Techniques

In drying plants, botanists often dry themselves.
Dry words and dry facts will not fire hearts.
                                        - John Muir

Voyageur Program   Courtesy of Pictured Rocks National Lakeshore

The most successful programs are fresh and original. Actors, story-tellers, preachers, and film makers all provide sources of inspiration.

Some popular ways to convey an interpretive message are:

Characterization - Using either a historic personality or an imaginary creature who can give insight into a topic.

Storytelling - The age old method of handing down history and passing along values to others.

Guided Imagery - Using "mental field trips" to take audiences to places far away or perhaps too dangerous to visit in person.

Puppetry - Finger puppets to larger than life creatures can make abstract concepts understandable and fun.

Using Live Animals - One of the most memorable of all experiences for an audience. There can be problems if not well planned.

Characterization

Costumed Interpretation

The decision to do costumed interpretation as a character or as yourself depends on the context of the program. Many historic sites find that role playing characters is too limiting. Interpreters conducting historic site tours or cultural demonstrations may better serve the visitor by simply being themselves. This "third person" interpretation has several advantages.

• In third person, you can answer questions only a contemporary could know. A first-person character, being from another era, would have to feign ignorance to stay in character.

• Third person interpretation may be less intimidating to visitors.

• In third person interpretation, the costume serves as a prop, lending credibility to the cultural information presented.

• First person interpretation requires theatric skill to be believable.

• First person interpretation requires another person to "set the scene" and prepare the audience to meet someone from the past.

If, however, the audience can be prepared and the scene set, characterization may be the best choice. A character can sweep us away to another time. Characters engage the imagination and evoke a whole range of emotions - humor, drama, pathos.

Characters humanize events and concepts, making them personal and real to visitors. You don't need a Shakespearean production, simply inform your visitors with dramatic and provocative situations.

LBJ Ranch National Historic Site, TX, Michael Gross
Ranch life is demonstrated at a chuck wagon. Since visitors are freely roaming the site, third person interpretation is the best choice.

Fort McHenry, Maryland   Warren Bielenberg
An 1814 private explains his musket. If done in character, these children may have felt intimidated by him. In third person, the interpreter can engage them in a friendly dialog.

Fort Scott, Kansas   Warren Bielenberg
An 1842 first sergeant is portrayed. A brief encounter with an historic character adds a new dimension to visitor's appreciation of the site.

Ike Ferris, River Pilot

There are mountains of facts and statistics compiled about the logging era in the Great Lakes states. These facts are not inherently interesting, and can be downright boring. The interpreter's challenge is to make them "come alive."

The Wisconsin River was a major corridor into the "Pinery" in the last century. Each winter trees were felled on the tributaries and later floated on spring floods to the boom towns and sawmills down river. Prairie sodbusters as far away as Iowa and Nebraska demanded all the white pine that could be floated to them. A hearty breed of men like Ike Ferris risked their lives to raft rough-cut planks down the surging Wisconsin.

Visitors can re-live these times through the eyes of an Ike Ferris. He can step out of the past and share his dreams with the visitors. Wet to the knees, hands calloused and rope-burned, reeking of tobacco, and with an adventurous sparkle in his eyes, he speaks the language of the river in a booming voice.

Ike Ferris, 19th Century Wisconsin River Lumberraft Pilot   Doug Moore

Preparing the Audience to Meet a Character

One nature center used Ike Ferris to share the history of the Wisconsin River with their community. A Sunday excursion began with a general information session followed by a trip to the river. The naturalist led the group through a forest down granite cliffs to the edge of the rushing river. The group settled back on sun-warmed, ancient boulders.

Prepare Your Audience

- Make the audience comfortable. If outdoors, the sun and wind should not be in their faces.

- Background information must be provided so the audience is prepared for the character when he appears.

- Place the audience in a setting that makes them receptive to the character.

- When you scout your area for "stages," do so at different times of the day and in different lighting conditions. The correct angle of the sun can turn a clearing into a sun-speckled cathedral.

- Sounds and smells are important mood setters. The sound of rushing water provides a pleasing backdrop, but not if it drowns out the speaker. Recorded sounds can work well indoors, but can seem artificial out-of-doors.

"These five billion year old rocks have been polished by water and ice for millennia. A mere hundred and twenty-five years ago this was the feared Shaurette Rapids. Citizens from our town lined the banks to cheer the river rafters through these treacherous rapids. Many a young man lost his life for a few dollars. It's too bad there are no rafters alive today to tell us what it was like to take a 'rapids piece' through Shaurette Rapids."

A looming figure suddenly appears on the rocks above the group, backlit by the sun. "Bullroar," he bellows. "The river never got Ike Ferris. I'll tell you what it was like to run rapids pieces down the Wisconsin." He scrambles nimbly down the rocks, for an old man, positions himself on a rock with the river rushing behind him and scrutinizes the group.

Wet to the knees, Ike pushes his felt hat far back on his forehead. Pipe lit, thumbs thrust through his suspenders, he begins to spin yarns of his days on the river.

Historic photo of a 19th century Wisconsin River pilot
Develop characters from old photos and documents.

Stage Dramatic Entrances

- Always select a stage, for example, a stump, a hill, a stream, or an old piece of farm equipment.
- The character's first words should capture the audience.
- The character's physical presence should dominate.
- The character's actions should be as carefully conceived as his words.

Creating Authentic Characters

For a rafter like Ike Ferris, limit **props** to a gold watch and chain draped across his hip, and a horse tended by a young boy. Ike's livelihood depended on the number of runs he could make in a day. "I use my horse to gig back to the head of the rapids," Ike explains, alluding to the horse grazing on the bank above them.

Authentic props and tools can add to the drama of any characterization. A double bitted axe can turn a grocery clerk into a lumberjack. A watch and chain can take you back a hundred years. A wrist watch can return you to the present just as abruptly. Be authentic to the period.

Props are fascinating to visitors. A spark from flint and steel fanned into flames is captivating. An old cowpoke becomes credible when he rolls a cigarette and slurps coffee from a chipped enamel cup. **Attention to character detail** is essential.

Small personal touches can put the final stamp of credibility on a character. A lumberjack's hands must be calloused and strong. A pioneer woman must have hands that are rough with worn fingernails. A teamster should have leather-stained palms. A rafter should be wet to the knees. Study dirt on people working. The face is seldom dirty, but the neck and hands often are. Perspiration can add to the effect if not overdone.

Ways to Create Authentic Characters

- **Clothing** should be comfortable and show signs of wear and appropriate soiling. Clothing should not look like a costume used only for productions, but should be a natural extension of the character, something the character lives in and works in.

- **Make-up,** if applied at all, should be used lightly. Interpretive characters are usually seen at close range. Make-up may look artificial.

- **Sounds and smells** add to the total effect. Stale beer, cigar smoke, and banjo music are part of a turn-of-the-century tavern. Fresh coffee brewing on a pot-bellied stove adds human appeal to a country store.

- **Lighting** can be the single most important visual effect. Don't leave it to chance. Kerosene lanterns and candles can enhance a story. Indoors, two or three small spotlights with dimmer switches will probably be adequate to illuminate the character. Side light with cool colors on one side and warm on the other will add depth to an interpreter's face. Good lighting should call attention to the subject, not to itself.

Developing Real Characters

Develop individuals, not stereotypes. Think of a character as a real individual with past experiences and inner motivations. What makes your character unique from similar personalities?

For example, a "tavern keeper" might give an adequate portrayal of life in a Wisconsin lumber town in the 1870's. But a more colorful perspective could be shared by a tavern keeper named Leo Glinski, a Polish immigrant who has operated the tavern since 1857.

Draw on your experience to develop your personalities. Use your own life to gain empathy with a character. Ask yourself, "Why is this character in a particular situation? What does he or she hope to accomplish by interacting with the group?

Ask questions like these while developing a character: Who am I? What is my family role? How do I

sound? What mannerisms do I have? What is my background? My temperament? My usual posture? My physical features? What am I most interested in? How am I like or unlike the audience?

When planning your character, **think in terms of actions, not words.** A voyageur straining under a load of pelts groans and grunts as he drops the pelts on the shore. These sounds would mean little on paper, but add a lot to the performance. Visualize the action and then record it.

Choose characters who would know about the time period or concepts to be interpreted. Avoid famous personalities. The visitor has preconceived notions about Abe Lincoln and Eleanor Roosevelt. It is better to interpret these people through a minor participant like President Lincoln's coachman or Eleanor Roosevelt's secretary.

Ike Ferris grave site on the banks of the Wisconsin River   Michael Gross

Wisconsin history describes river pilots as flamboyant pillars of Wisconsin River lumber towns. They were the leaders of 20 or more men who rafted the year's work of a lumber mill to markets on the Mississippi. A river pilot portrayal should convey the confidence of a leader.

Some Memorable Characters

The Firefighter

The audience was seated, expectations rising. The interpreter entered the room wearing a yellow hard hat and carrying a soot-stained axe.

He was soot stained, too. Black smudges streaked his cheeks and hands. His disheveled clothing smelled of ash. The group had no trouble recognizing him as a firefighter. They watched the firefighter spread dry pine needles and gray sticks on the floor. They watched nervously as he poured "kerosene" (vanilla extract diluted in water) over the kindling.

"Fire" was the topic. It seemed particularly timely given the hot summer day. Prolonged dry spells had increased the danger of uncontrollable burns, the interpreter said. He then described factors that increased fire danger.

During the talk he held a long burning matchstick. "A fire," he said, suspensefully drawing the orange flame toward the kindling, "can start just like..." But just before the interpreter ignited the pine needles and gray sticks, he would remember another point to share. He always drew the flame away in the nick of time.

The interpreter never did light the kindling. After telling his story of fire, he glanced at his watch. "Holy smoke!" he exclaimed, "I've got to help the boys down at the east pass. I was supposed to be there ten minutes ago." The firefighter grabbed his axe and fled the room.

People pay attention to the familiar...a firefighter. Authenticity fosters believability...a soot stained axe and clothing smelling of ash. Suspense and movement capture attention...he drew the flame toward the kindling. People pay attention to things that affect them...like the threat of fire on a hot summer day.

The Night Spirit

The group chatted happily as they followed a path lit by votive lights into the dark woods. The path led them to an outdoor amphitheater where an interpreter seated them.

The interpreter began a discussion about creatures of the night when a second figure suddenly appeared from behind the group. She walked in front of them. Clad in fur skins and carrying a flaming torch, the surprise character introduced herself as the Night Spirit of Sunset Woods.

The Spirit shrilly asked, "Why are you making so much noise?" She then told them of the things they could see if they walked quietly. Occasionally, she would draft a "volunteer" to help her demonstrate a concept.

The Spirit stayed with the group for only ten minutes. She vanished back into the woods after sharing her message, leaving the first interpreter to continue on the night walk with the group.

A dramatic entry is enhanced when the character is introduced by a second interpreter. Votive lights set the mood. The Spirit entered mysteriously from a point clearly separate from the route the group has followed...and vanished just as mysteriously.

The Rose Hip

One interpreter drew on his experiences foraging for wild fruits to develop an imaginary rose-hip character. The character, once a man, had turned into a giant rose hip after eating the red fruits to survive one winter.

A six-foot high rose-hip dashes into the room. Breathless and tense, the character whispered an explanation to the group; he was on the run from a jelly factory that wanted to can him. He had seen the room's open door and ran inside to hide.

The rose-hip did not just feel worried, he showed it. The character's physique and personality, red tights, and bulging torso surprised the group. They had expected one thing, but were presented with something completely different.

The Surly Surveyor

Surveyors opened North America to development. As they parceled the land into grids, they carefully recorded features of the landscape. Through the eyes of the Surly Surveyor, we experience the changes from wilderness to cityscape.

The Surly Surveyor, Rob Nurre of Wisconsin, adapts his character to each community in which he performs. This requires local survey notes and information on the person who recorded them. At Cuyahoga Valley National Recreation Area, the Surly Surveyor becomes Seth Pease, assistant to surveyor Moses Cleveland, namesake for Cleveland, Ohio.

The Surly Surveyor

Doug Moore

Storytelling

"Modern-day storytellers perform an ancient role in society: telling stories to entertain, teach, transmit culture, and interpret value systems. We all need to hear and tell stories from world cultures to share in the universality of human emotions that unfold in each tale."

Bert and Noel MacCarry
Legacy, March/April, 1991

Storytelling is a powerful interpretive technique. Stories arouse emotions and interest about history and nature. They humanize and give insight into otherwise sterile subjects. For example, the study of the westward expansion can be a dull recitation of dates, acts of Congress, and faceless names. Or, it can be experienced through stories of men like Jim Bridger, a mountain man who lived these significant events and who shows us what we have lost through the taming of the wilderness.

Every culture has storytelling traditions which teach values, attitudes, and philosophies. These cultural insights are best appreciated when shared through the oral traditions of their people.

The Council for American Indian Interpretation

Photo by Bob Belous, Courtesy of S.W. Region, National Park Service

The "Storyteller" figurine, symbol of the CAII, is an image of an elder, a tradition bearer, with rapt children gathered around.

The CAII is an affiliated section of the National Association of Interpretation. Years ago some interpreters realized that it was difficult to share the spiritual and world views of Native Americans through conventional means. The CAII was formed to promote and develop cultural interpretation using traditional methods.

Stories were the principle method of education and entertainment. *"From the stories told, young people learned of their origins and history. Their language became beautiful and intimate. Through story, they mapped their homeland, its trails, shrines, and places of great happenings. They pictured the actions and learned the habits of animals, which in due course, would agree to be hunted, if the hunter knew the rituals of respect."*

William E. Brown
Legacy, December, 1990

Tips for Storytelling

- Select stories that mean something to you and that you like to tell. Good stories relate to a group's common experiences. Good stories pose a problem that cause listeners to anticipate a resolution.

- Select stories that are relevant to your interpretive goals. For instance, you might choose one that has an environmental message.

- Research the facts of the story. You have to know your subject to do more than simply entertain. For example, you should understand Indian culture and religion if you tell Coyote stories.

- Select a point of view. Will you tell the story from an omniscient perspective in the third person or in the first person as if it happened to you? Sometimes you can refresh a stale story by retelling it from a different vantage point. The story of *The Three Little Pigs* by A. Wolf is a good example of a revised classic.

- Memorize a sequence of images for the story, but not necessarily the words.
  - Read the story aloud (if from a written source).
  - Next, visualize the story. Imagine the plot revealed as a series of photographs. Picture the key images you want to share.
  - You may, at this point, write an outline to refresh your memory later.

- When telling the story, keep the listener's imagination engaged with sequential images:
  - Use voice inflection that fits the action.
  - Use gestures to paint images.
  - Recreate sounds for dramatic effect: The "crrreak" of a door, the "zzzzzt" of a mosquito landing on someone's nose.
  - Create distinct characters and have them speak to each other. Use dialects, if appropriate. Misuse of cultural dialects can be insulting to others.

- Use frequent pauses so the imagery can unfold. Avoid going more than 10-12 syllables without a pause. However, do so at random so there is no distracting pattern. Hold pauses longer to create suspense.

- Storytelling is an intimate medium. Everyone should feel that you are talking directly to them. Make random eye contact and focus on individuals.

- Avoid using props. Imagery is the storyteller's tool. When props are used, listeners focus on them rather than the story.

- Stick to the point. Avoid over-illustrating and telling too many details.

- Believe in yourself. If your body language is stiff and lacks confidence, your audience will perceive it. Enjoy what you are doing and the audience will too.

Storytelling Cautions

- Talking in a monotone.

- Using a fake or affected voice.

- Talking too fast or meandering verbally.

- Using limp or repetitive gestures.

- Insulting other cultures.

- Teaching misinformation about nature.

- Over-anthropomorphizing wildlife.

- Telling stories you don't like.

Northlands Storytelling Annual Conference, Elkader, Iowa   Susan Gilchrist

Stories often explain why things are the way they are. We all like stories that we can relate to our own experiences or that help us better understand our own world.

Here are a few sources of stories recommended by Susan Gilchrist, a storyteller.

American Folk Tales and Legends, retold by Neil Grant, includes stories of frontier heroes, engineers and steelmen, Indian myths and legends, sailors' yarns and fishy tales, animal yarns, the wild West, strange tales, superheroes like Paul Bunyan, witches and other devilry.

Earthmaker's Tales, by Gretchen Will Mayo, includes North American Indian stories about Earth happenings.

Keepers of the Earth, by Michael J. Caduto and Joseph Bruchac, includes both Native American stories and environmental activities for teaching children.

Themes cover creation; fire; earth; wind and weather; water; sky; seasons; plants and animals; life, death, spirit; and unity of earth.

The Tree In the Moon and Other Legends of Plants and Trees, by Rosalind Kerven, a collection of eleven stories from around the world.

Why The Possum's Tale is Bare and Other North American Indian Nature Tales, collected by James E. Connolly. This short collection contains tales from eastern woodland, western plains, and coastal tribes.

Wildflower Folklore and *Garden Flower Folklore,* both by Laura C. Martin, offer brief mini-tales about specific flowers, excellent fare for the interpreter starving for stories.

Guided Imagery

Guided imagery transports people to distant places or times. An interpreter can take a group back to the Battle of Gettysburg or inside a beehive. With guided imagery you can even explore places that would be too dangerous in real life, like the abandoned tunnels of an old copper mine. Descriptive language acts as the starting point in "fantasy trips." Each individual's imagination then takes over.

At a workshop exploring the Wisconsin River an interpreter wanted to reveal the human relationship to the river over time. To travel through time, the group would journey by canoe downstream. They would stop at islands to meet characters from the past like Jesuit "black robes" and lumberjacks. They would see wild ginseng and river otter. But how could the group understand how the river has changed?

A guided imagery experience seemed the best way to share these changes. It helped visitors perceive the river not only as a flow of water, but as a river of time.

Research and Script Writing

Research is the first step in developing a fantasy trip. You need to know the past you plan to describe.

When writing the script, imagine the scenes, and write down the sensory and visual images. Create specific images that relate to our common experiences.

Wisconsin River   Ron Zimmerman
Choosing the location for a fantasy trip is important. This quiet spot offers a full view of the winding blue water. In this case, the group took their trip on a large granite rock near the river.

Beginning a Trip

Begin a guided imagery trip by inviting people to sit in a comfortable place. Help them to relax and to set aside distracting thoughts (e.g., have them look into the flowing water and drift with the river back in time).

The following script was used to help the visitor imagine past life along the Wisconsin River. It sets the stage for a character interpretation by a Jesuit priest.

Human History on the Wisconsin River - A Guided Imagery

As you sit on these ancient granite rocks polished by ice and water, gaze into the dark current and drift back 10,000 years. Across the river, just out of view, stands a massive wall of ice, higher than the tallest tree, and stretching for thousands of miles to the Arctic Circle. The water in the river runs milky green with powdered rock from the glacier.

At the edge of the glacier, you see dark haired people wearing animal skins surrounding a furry elephant-like creature. They sling spears into its underbelly.

The river drifts on through the centuries. The climate warms, the great ice sheet melts. The conical reflection of spruce trees in the river is replaced by the bright autumn glow of maple trees. A band of Winnebagos are making wigwams for their winter sugar camp.

After the season of the popping trees, early spring to us, they tap the trees with bone drills and insert hollow sumac stems. Hissing hot stones in hide-lined, sap-filled holes give off the sweet aroma of maple sugar. Children play noisily with snow snakes, carved sticks that they send skidding down ice-lined trenches. They happily talk in a tongue you do not understand.

They stop abruptly and run excitedly to the water. Far up river, coming down stream, is a black-robed figure in a birch bark canoe, paddled by men of another tribe. (At this point, a black-robed Jesuit priest appears in a canoe from behind an island singing in French. The fantasy trip ends, and a characterization of Jesuit exploration on the Wisconsin River begins.)

Sharing Trips

The guided imagery trip is a communication technique that inspires creative thinking. It is a quiet activity that depends on trust between an interpreter and a group. An interpreter suggests specific, accurate images, letting each person visualize his own experience.

By sharing experiences, people gain greater insights into their own attitudes toward a natural resource. They can also gain insights from the ideas of others.

Ask questions like: How did you envision the clothing of the people? How did the banks of the river change? Were the men or the women boiling the sap?

Tips for Guided Imagery

- Use guided imagery to transport people to a time and place where they cannot physically go.

- Research your subject to create accurate images.

- Develop a script that relates the sequential images in story form (see tips for storytelling).

- Place your audience in a setting conducive to entering their imagination. Create a peaceful, trusting atmosphere.

- Use good storytelling technique to guide the group through the experience. Take lots of time, use long pauses, to allow people to visualize the scene.

- Have the group share their experience.

Puppet Interpretation

Puppets are an invitation to enter a fantasy world where anything is possible. Trees can talk, spirits can materialize, and wild animals can be safely petted.

Even adults welcome the chance to see their world in new and involving ways. There are many uses for puppets. Put a puppet to work in your program.

Courtesy of Marti Kane, North Carolina Wildlife Resources Commission

Baldy, the recycling vulture, encourages people to recycle. He holds up trash items in his beak as the audience suggests ways to recycle them. He sniffs the audience to see if anyone is dead. Periodic hand waving reminds this "slow" vulture that everyone is still alive.

Advantages to Using Puppets

- They command center stage.

- They **interact** with the audience. Participation and two way communication can be maximized.

- Complex concepts and abstract ideas can be physically interpreted with puppets.

- They can present controversial issues in humorous nonthreatening ways.

- They are three dimensional. They work without electricity or expensive buildings. They can emerge spontaneously from a knapsack.

- They require minimal maintenance. They withstand physical abuse and torment without suffering.

- They are inexpensive to create and easily stored.

- They behave in predictable ways. Unlike real animals, they don't bite, excrete, or hide unless you want them to.

Carpet Foam Creatures of the Minnesota Zoo

Courtesy of Minnesota Zoo Skytrail; Text by Elizabeth Heidorn, Photos by Marsha Knittig

Skytrail naturalists at the Minnesota Zoo have discovered that carpet foam, the spongy layer usually found under the carpet, can be transformed into anything from masks to moose to 80 foot monsters.

Originally a theater medium, carpet foam is affordable, easy and fun to use. The resulting props are big and bold for easy viewing in crowded zoo buildings or from the monorail cars.

Carpet foam props get attention as a talking tree for Arbor Day, a sea star at the coal reef exhibit, or a big brown bat for Halloween. Programs tailored to the event and the audience hold that attention. Always a careful mix of conservation, education, and fun, the message supports the mission of the Minnesota Zoo: strengthen the bond between people and living earth.

The list of carpet foam props includes a scaled-down Skytrail cab; skittering cockroaches; a two-person moose; marsh monsters with flexible, clawed paws; a finely-feathered owl; fluorescent prehistoric fish; an ana-tomically correct crayfish; a jellyfish; an aluminum can that tells tall can tales (and urges people to recycle).

Carpet foam comes in rolls, like carpet, and is sold by the foot in a variety of thicknesses at building supply stores. The 3/8 inch twilight foam has proven to be the most versatile.

Carpet foam is strong enough to hold its shape without underlying support; yet it can be cut with a household scissors. Cut edges, or any two foam surfaces to be joined, are coated with contact cement. In a minute, the cement becomes tacky and the edges/surfaces are joined in a permanent bond. The carpet foam will accept enamel, latex, or watercolor paint without further preparation.

The finished props are lightweight, flexible, and can be worn comfortably. Since they are used over and over again, it is important that they are able to be folded flat and stored easily.

The ideas for props and costumes come from many different sources,

Creative costumes like the "talking tree" are used in educational presentations on Arbor Day, Earth Day, and conservation days.

everything from magazine covers to traditional sewing patterns to Peterson field guides.

Skytrail naturalists have developed patterns and "how-to" videos; and "hands-on" workshops are available at the Minnesota Zoo. For more information, call or write: Elizabeth Heidorn, Education Department, Minnesota Zoo, 13000 Zoo Blvd., Apple Valley, MN 55124, telephone (612) 431-9222.

This sucker-studded sea star, using its expandable stomach, discusses its feeding behavior with visitors by the coral reef shark exhibit.

This bull moose gives Skytrail naturalists an opportunity to talk about adaptations and animal management.

Monterey Bay Aquaravan

Photos and text courtesy of Dr. Pat Rutowski, Outreach Education © 1991, Monterey Bay Aquarium

The Monterey Bay Aquarium's mobile Aquaravan carries 300 gallons of water in a running seawater system and tidepool creatures including sea stars, anemones, and crabs. In addition to live animals, the staff uses costumes, puppets, and theatrical techniques to interpret the ocean environment.

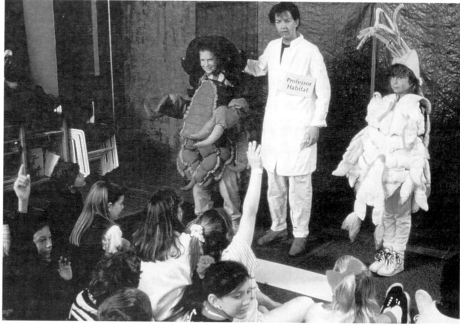

In a school assembly, Professor Habitat assisted by two eager students dressed as a rock crab and sand crab, tries to determine which crab is adapted to live in which habitat

In "Seashore Friends," Freddie the Fish introduces students to his tidepool buddies.

The imaginative nature of preschool and primary school children lends itself to the use of puppets and pantomimes in teaching about animal behavior. A gardening glove with a shell and legs painted on it becomes a hermit crab puppet and a sock spiked with purple pipe cleaner spines nods gently as the sea urchin puppet. Foam covered with felt creates the sea star puppet whose mouth and retractible chiffon stomach are revealed when the puppet is turned over.

(Right) Deep sea animals come to life as the outreach staff dons lantern fish and angler fish costumes in "Deep Side Story."

School assembly programs are 30 to 45 minutes long, while public event skits at fairs last only 15 or 20 minutes, about as long as an audience will stay in a festival setting. Dressups invite audience participation. Quick appearances of many animal characters catch and hold the attention of passersby.

Costumes and puppets can easily and effectively be incorporated into any interpretive program. Mattress foam is inexpensive and the technology to mold it into animal shapes is relatively simple.

(Left) Youngsters dress as squids school together to fight off Shark Vader in a public event skit called "Squids in Space."

(Above) A member of the Aquaravan staff wears a whale costume to teach about migration, the differences between mammals and fish, and the history of whaling. Complete with baleen, whale lice and blowhole, this costume lacks only the ability to spout.

Ten Steps to a Puppet Program
(As adapted from the Minnesota Zoo Skytrail Programs)

- Identify the issue or concept for interpretation.

- Identify the situation in which this idea is best presented (special event, school class orientation, to introduce live animals, etc.).

- Identify your audience. How will they relate to a puppet show? What interests do they have?

- Write a one-sentence theme/goal statement clearly defining the program.

- Define objectives for visitor response:
  - What will the audience learn?
  - How will they feel?

- What audience reactions are you seeking?

- Identify an appropriate site for your puppet show. Consider how that site may affect your presentation.

- Make lists of needed props, timetables, and assignments.

- Develop a script. Make or select your puppets.

- Rehearse the performance, fine-tune timing and script.

- Evaluate the "live" performance and modify it for the future.

Some Simple Puppet Characters You Can Make

"Jaws" is a shark made from instrument-packaging foam and cloth.

Photos by Doug Moore

"Ranger Ron" has a head of papier mache with glued foam for facial features.

Three socks and a scarf tell the butterfly story. Knot the scarf in the shape of a butterfly and put it in your fist. Then put on the crysalis sock (brown), catterpillar sock (green), and egg sock (white).

Tips for Using Hand Puppets

- Move the puppets mouth "in sync" with what it is saying.

- Open the mouth as the words begin. "Don't bite them" off. Open and close the mouth with each syllable. Practice in front of a mirror.

- Move the lower jaw. Don't "flip the lid." The head should remain level as the lower jaw moves.

- Stay in character. Don't spoil the impression that the puppet is alive.

- Puppets should make eye contact with the audience. Sweep eyes across the audience, occasionally resting on one place.

- Let the puppets "carry the program." Don't lecture with a puppet on your hand.

Courtesy of St. Croix National Scenic Riverway

- Develop a distinct personality and voice for each puppet character. The more unlike you the puppet sounds and acts, generally the more successful the illusion.

- Keep the program short and active. "Leave the audience wanting more"...not relieved that a long program has finally ended. Five-ten minutes on stage is usually adequate for any character.

- Look at your puppet when it is talking. You must believe in the "realness" of your characters if the audience is expected to. Be a good listener!

- Develop a story.

Using Live Animals

A live animal can be an unforgettable addition to your program. Animals are dynamic and unpredictable. People like to see creatures up-close that they may not see otherwise. Live animals are a catalyst for real understanding, because they offer the chance to learn facts while experiencing them.

Certain animals can cope with groups of people better than others. Before planning a program that involves a live animal, find out which ones these are. A barred owl, for example, is usually more docile than a great horned owl. Fox snakes are easier to handle than water snakes. Research the animal's habits and needs. Conservation officers, animal rehabilitators, and zoo personnel can give you practical insights. Books, including those listed in the Resources section, will also tell you how to properly care for a captive animal.

Know the law. Unless you purchase an animal from a pet store, you usually need a permit to have a native species, even for a short time. Just as important, be sure to have the proper facilities, nutritious food sources and time to keep the animal in good health. Keeping an animal as a permanent guest of a nature center means a long term commitment. Consider instead short-term captivity and release. An animal can certainly be a valuable educational tool, but its primary value is the role it plays in nature.

Everglades National Park, Florida   Michael Gross

In "Snakes Alive," species common to south Florida are presented. Visitors learn about varieties of poisonous and non-poisonous snakes, where they are found and what they eat. Most important, they are given the message that snakes are not animals to fear and loathe.

Mammoth Cave National Park, Kentucky   Warren Bielenberg

A "Birds of Prey" program brings visitors up close to seldom seen and often misunderstood birds. Adaptations for predation can be easily admired.

Planning a Program With a Live Animal

A seven-foot bull snake or a powerful raptor like a bald eagle is the biggest "pow" your program can have. Live animals will always "steal the show" and provoke questions as soon as they are seen. You will, quite simply, be upstaged!

Keep your guest concealed until after you have set expectations. Ask for the group's help in developing a calm, peaceful atmosphere. A soft voice, as well as soft lighting, helps an animal feel secure.

If you choose to handle the animal during a program, be sure to practice beforehand with someone who has experience. Have the proper equipment - a snake bag, for example, or heavy gloves to protect your hands from sharp talons. Have a suitable cage handy, too. Visitors will learn as much from how you treat the animal as from what you say about it.

Tips for Live Animal Programs

- Set expectations for audience behavior and respect for the animal before it arrives on stage.

- Never endanger an animal's health or well-being. Handling of the animal by the audience should be limited. The interpreter should control the animal. If it shows stress, stop.

- Stress the fact that wild animals require special care, that they are not pets. Explain why they have been removed from the wild for this program.

- Protect people from harm from the animals.

- Prepare for the unexpected.

- Have a talk prepared: theme, pow-bridge-body-conclusion.

- Avoid humanizing animals (such as using pet names) as this creates misconceptions about its role in the wild.

- Demonstrate and explain natural animal behaviors.

- Although facts about the biology of the animal are important, it is just as important to relate the role of the animal in an ecosystem.

Interpret "Ordinary" Animals

Even common creatures are wondrous things. Daddy-long-legs, for example, are not really spiders at all. They protect themselves with stink glands near the base of their front legs. They even do push-ups!

Why not develop a program about "creepy crawlies," and involve some of the subjects as live, featured guests? Other small creatures like ticks, mosquitoes, and various beetles are easily accessible. For a wetland theme, crayfish, frogs and water boatmen are fascinating subjects.

Warren County Conservation Area, Iowa   Kathleen Regnier

Farm animals and pond creatures fascinate people if they have never experienced them. Interpretive programs can seize on this interest to teach ecology and give insight about where food comes from.

Zoo Shows

With so much to see and do, zoo shows must be short, fast paced, and entertaining.

Zoo programs must not present humanized caricatures of animals. Instead, natural behaviors are displayed. Narration adds to an understanding and respect for the animals.

Photos of San Diego Wild Animal Park, California
Michael Gross

During a bird show, a golden eagle is induced to open its wings. The interpreter explains the significance of this behavior and provides fascinating facts about the bird.

Following the show, visitors are invited to a "Hawk Talk" for a closer look at the birds and an opportunity to get their questions answered.

In "Animals of North America" common mammals are featured. A raccoon is given food which it takes to a pond to wash. The significance of this behavior is explained.

The "tools" of a predator are shown on a bobcat.

Seasonal Animal Programs

Knowing the seasonal migrations in your area can provide program ideas, too. Monarch butterflies and American woodcock are just two common animals that are easily observed. Do you know when chorus frogs and spring peepers call from their breeding ponds?

A bird banding program during spring or fall migrations promises the chance to see birds up close. If you are not a licensed bird-bander, find someone in your area who is. Together you can plan a program that will teach bird lore, ecology, and conservation.

Photos courtesy of Chugach National Forest, Alaska

Proper handling and banding of a bird is demonstrated.

Proper technique of weighing a bird is demonstrated. The purpose of weighing a bird is explained.

The opportunity to touch a bird before it is released is an experience that will never be forgotten by this young visitor.

6
Trail Techniques

The essence is to travel gracefully rather than to arrive.
- Enos Mills

Everglades National Park, Florida

Michael Gross

It's 9:00 a.m. A January sun warms and evaporates the morning dew. The interpreter takes his place overlooking seventy-five eager visitors seated in open gondola cars. The Shark Valley Tram is about to begin its first run of the day into the heart of Florida's Everglades.

"Welcome to Shark Valley. Are you ready for our river cruise? Oh, you didn't know we were on a river.

"Well, this is unlike any river you've ever seen. There is nothing like it anywhere else in the world. Today, I want to share with you the reasons this place is so special."

The interpreter leaves his seat and walks to a carpet covered inclined table placed on the pavement that all can see.

Picking up a pail of water he says, "What will happen when I pour this water on the table? Right! The water will spread out and slowly flow off the south end."

He demonstrates this, then pulls a large map of the Everglades from his knapsack. "The Shark River begins 60 miles north of here where Lake Okeechobee overflows its banks.

Everglades National Park   Michael Gross

The water spreads like a sheet into a river 50 miles wide. After only one hundred miles, it flows into the Gulf of Mexico. The slope is so gentle it may take a whole year before the water completes its journey."

"I know you're here to see the wildlife. Let's start our cruise and see what's on the river this morning."

The tram begins its slow journey on the twelve mile loop road. Binoculars scan the landscape and cameras click as herons and ibises gracefully rise in front of the approaching vehicle. The interpreter joins in the visitors' excitement by calling out each new sighting.

After a mile or so, the tram stops. The interpreter leaps to the ground and slogs into the river. "Who wants to join me? I want to show you the most important citizens of the Everglades." He reaches down and hauls up a handful of the matted green material lying on the lime-stone bedrock. "Everyone, reach down and grab a handful. This doesn't look like much, but if it weren't for this, you wouldn't be seeing herons and ibises this morning. This is called periphyton. It's a collection of mostly algae that forms the base of the Everglades."

Reaching into his knapsack, the interpreter pulls out a handful of posterboard illustrations. "I need some volunteers." The poster pictures are passed out. "Now we need to arrange these into an Everglades food chain. We have here (pointing to a grinning volunteer) periphyton. What eats the periphyton? (mosquitoes, apple snails) What feeds on apple snails? (kites) What feeds on mosquitoes? (frogs) What feeds on frogs and fish? (bigger fish, alligators, herons) And so you see, this periphyton is pretty important stuff. It starts this whole chain."

The tram soon approaches a large pool of water on the side of the road. A ten-foot alligator lies at the back of the pool. "Who would like to wrestle that gator?" A young man raises his hand with a grin. "First let me show you what that gator will do to you." The interpreter grabs the volunteer by the foot. "He'll grab you by the leg and spin around and around (feigning a spinning motion) and hold you under water till you drown. Then, in a few days after you rot, he'll come back and eat you piece by piece. Still want to wrestle him?" (No!)

"If it weren't for the gators, it would be pretty hard for Everglades' wildlife to survive the dry season. This gator keeps the hole open by bulldozing out the bottom. During the winter when the rains stop, this might be the only water deep enough for fish, turtles, and frogs. And where you find fish, you find otters and herons. Now that gator will collect a tax for the service it provides. So critters coming for lunch at the gator hole had better watch it so they don't become his lunch!"

At the farthest point of the loop, a tall tower stands overlooking the Everglades. A thirty minute stop allows the visitors to look out over the "river of grass" and drink in its beauty. The interpreter sets up a spotting scope on a group of feeding whitetail deer. Curiosity draws in a crowd of people. The interpreter encourages everyone to keep their eyes open for other wildlife.

Back on the road, the tram enters a forested island. "Did anyone's ears pop? Welcome to one of South Florida's mountains. Actually, we are only about four feet above sea level, but this little rise is enough to invite a whole new community of plants and animals. These islands are called 'hammocks' which means 'garden place.' They are truly gardens with palms and mahogany trees, ferns and orchids, tree snails and snakes. You may even find a panther here.

"When you were on the tower, did you see how these hammocks are shaped like a teardrop? Why would they be shaped like that?" (The flowing water has shaped the islands through the centuries.)

The tram rumbles on through flocks of marsh birds and finally returns to the ranger station. "Before you go, there's one story the National Park Service wants you to know. The Everglades is the most threatened park in the national park system."

"The water no longer flows clearly or freely from Lake Okeechobee. Although we saw a lot of wildlife today, it isn't nearly as abundant as it once was. And unless a whole lot of people show they care, we will lose the rest."

"You can help by supporting development limits on south Florida. Support the purchase of critical lands. Support the dechannelization of the Kissimee River above Lake Okeechobee. Support less diversion of water to Miami and the Atlantic coast. Without your help, there will be no River of Grass in the future."

Everglades National Park, Florida   Michael Gross
Visitors are invited to "squeeze the periphyton" as they walk in the "River of Grass."

The Everglades tram tour illustrates several techniques which can be applied to any trail interpretation:

Interpret the Site

Here a complete story was told about the "River of Grass:" The uniqueness of sheet flow from Lake Okeechobee. The importance of all creatures in the food chain. The adaptations of wildlife to the dry season. Variation in the community caused by subtle factors. Most important, the visitor experienced the site in all its beauty and grandeur. No one will forget the warmth of the morning sun, the excitement of seeing abundant wildlife, and the beauty of the undeveloped landscape.

All trail interpretation should tell the story of the site. What makes a site unique? Become thoroughly familiar with its features. Know the plants and animals that live there. Become aware of seasonal cycles of different species. Know the cultural history.

Involve the Visitor

The more involved the visitor, the more memorable the experience. The Everglades interpreter involved the visitor in a number of ways. He gave concrete expression to abstract concepts through demonstrations and visual aids. He asked questions. He physically involved visitors by asking them to squeeze periphyton. He humorously and graphically illustrated what an alligator does to its prey. Colorful analogies made Florida mountains tangible.

Be a Host

Remember your "host" responsibilities:

Arrive at least 15 minutes early. Meeting people before the program begins can lend valuable insights into their interests and backgrounds.

Warmly welcome your audience. Introduce yourself, the walk theme, and the distance and time to be covered. Expectations must be set immediately. (Note: The Everglades interpreter did include this in his program.)

For latecomers, plan your first stop within view of the starting point. In this way, you can start on time yet still allow everyone to share the experience. Similarly, conclude your program at the original starting point. If you cannot make a loop trail or if you must conclude on the trail, at least return the visitors to the starting point.

Pace is also a consideration. Consider the whole group in pacing a walk. Assess the physical abilities of visitors. Move only as fast as the slowest walker.

Be aware of visitor discomfort. Have the sun shining in your eyes and wind blowing in your face, not the visitors'.

Tatra Mts. National Park, Poland   Michael Gross
Nature guiding is an old tradition in Europe. A rock is a stage to tell tales of the Tatras.

Plan Engaging Stops

At an interpretive stop the interpreter or an object is on center stage. Stops should always have a clear purpose. Examine each of the stops on the Everglades tram. What is the major concept presented at each? Do the techniques reveal the concept in an interpretive way?

Trail interpretation has been likened to a string of pearls. Each pearl is a gem of insight. The strand is held together by a thread of unity, a theme along which all of the pearls are strung. You must carefully prepare each pearl and its placement on the string, but the visitor should only perceive the whole necklace.

Most stops should be brief. Since a typical interpretive walk lasts about an hour, plan about five stops during your walk. Scenic views or

observation of wildlife may invite longer stops. Activity and interest will dictate the timing. Be sensitive to the interests of the group. Be aware of the bored members of the party as well as the eager ones. Move on before interest fades. Leave them wanting more.

Flexibility

Walks are challenging because unexpected things happen. If you have planned to stop at an alligator hole and if an otter suddenly appears, let the otter direct the program. Take advantage of the teachable moment by weaving the surprise into the theme of your program.

Unexpected natural events are not always welcome. Bad weather is a possibility. Have an alternate program in case of bad weather. Be cautious of advertising a program as "depending on weather." "Fair weather" is subject to the interpretation of each visitor.

Controlling Large Groups

Some programs attract especially large groups, perhaps thirty or more. Maintaining the interest of large numbers of people is a skill that comes with practice.

You must be the visible leader. Your group should resemble the orderly flight formation of Canada geese, not the random flocking of pigeons in a city park. Large groups require assertive leadership.

Wait for everyone to arrive at the stop before interpreting. When you interpret, speak audibly. Be sure that everyone can see both you and the object of attention. Often talking from a "stage" will accomplish this. One naturalist was leading a beaver walk along a creek. The banks were narrow and little room was available to the group around a stop. The naturalist walked into the stream to be clearly visible and audible to everyone. Stepping off the trail while

Apostle Islands National Lakeshore, Wisconsin   Michael Gross
"Life in the Boreal Forest" is the subject of this interpretive walk. The interpreter has positioned his group on the trail so that all can see the object of interest.

speaking to a group increases visibility, too. Standing on a rock or an incline can have the same effect. Look for "natural stages" to use on site.

Another technique in leading large groups is to lead half the group past the object to be interpreted. When you return to the object, the observers form a natural arc around it.

Walks usually combine planned and spontaneous interpretation. A firm understanding of the site, combined with enthusiasm, will help you create an enjoyable program.

Come Full Circle

Trail interpretation should make a circle thematically and physically. Each interpretive walk should begin and end at a common point.

Walks, like talks, have a beginning, middle, and end. The beginning and end should relate so that the audience has a sense of completeness. The stops develop the theme established in the beginning.

Mesa Verde National Park, NM   Michael Gross
Visitors are led into the ruins of the Anasazi in search of clues to a mysterious culture.

Gimmicks and Gadgets

Chugach National Forest, AK   Donna Zimmerman
A "gimmick bag," vest with lots of pockets, and a walking stick for pointing are useful tools for leading a walk.

Devices can make many ideas easier to understand. Gadgets can also involve the senses and serve as tools to focus attention.

Several props were used on the Shark Valley Tram. Sheet flow became understandable when a bucket of water was poured on an inclined table covered with carpet. Maps helped the visitor see a larger picture. Binoculars were aids for the senses.

Consider new possibilities: A simple walking stick can turn into a pointer that directs attention. A mirror focuses attention by reflecting light into a treetop cavity.

Naturalist Josh Barkin often placed little objects in a gold mining pan. This was his mini-stage for small objects and tiny actors. On one occasion, he used animal crackers to talk about endangered species.

Carry a gimmick bag filled with interpretive aids. Use your imagination. Gain inspiration from your local hardware store, grocery store, or flea market. Interpreters Mike Freed and David Shafer have a list of one hundred-forty items useful on the trail for interpreters. Their list is reproduced in the appendix.

Visitor Involvement on the Point Iroquois Lighthouse Tour

The process for planning an interpretive walk is similar to other types of interpretation. (See page 18 for the steps in planning the Point Iroquois Lighthouse Tour.)

Props, old photographs, imagery, physical interaction, and verbal participation through questioning all involve the Point Iroquois visitor. Active participation is key to an effective tour.

Point Iroquois Lighthouse, Hiawatha National Forest, Michigan   Michael Gross

Automatic lights in the shipping channel made the lighthouse and its keepers obsolete. The visitors are invited to view photos or read from journals at various points in the tour.

A volunteer is invited to stand on the spot where a small building once stood. Asked to speculate on what it was, visitors learn that a shed was here to store fuel for the light. Since lightning frequently struck the tower, fire was a constant danger.

Visitors read dramatic log entries such as rescues of sailors shipwrecked in Lake Superior storms.

Children are involved through questions: "Who do you think had to split and stack the firewood?" "How would you like having your schoolteacher living in your house with you?"

Themes for Trail Walks

Themes must be specific to the site. They should leave the visitor with the perception that the site they visited is special. Avoid generic "nature walks." Your title should reflect your theme and promise adventure. For example, a "swamp stomp" promises involvement while learning about that unique ecosystem.

Look for a fresh perspective on a topic. Avoid ho-hum predictability. Sometimes your destination is an exciting theme in itself: a falls, a mountain peak, an ancient tree. At other times, the anticipation of seeing exciting wildlife should get top billing. A hike to the "Bighorn Meadows," a "Whale Watch," or a "Moose in the Willows" walk will provide your theme. The following is a sampler of trail walks:

Big Cypress National Preserve, Florida   Michael Gross
A "swamp stomp" promises involvement while learning about a bald cypress swamp.

Photos courtesy of Pictured Rocks National Lakeshore
Walks in Pictured Rocks National Lakeshore interpret three themes about the site. Fragile and dynamic sand dunes are the subject of "Plant Communities of Grand Sable Dunes" (above, right). Violent storms and human dramas are interpreted in "Shipwrecks and Lighthouses" (left). Two wetland communities are contrasted in "Beach to Bog" (above, left).

(Right) A tour group enters the back porch of the Harry S. Truman home. People, not architectural details and room furnishings, are the real story. Tours through historic homes should connect people with their history. (Above) A walk through the neighborhood ties the Trumans to their community.

Photos courtesy of Harry S. Truman National Historic Site, Missouri

Imaginations are stimulated on a walk through the Effigy Mounds. The Little Bear effigy is a tangible connection to ancient Indians.

At Fire Point, the Mississippi River valley can be envisioned as it must have been when the mounds culture flourished here.

Photos courtesy of Effigy Mounds National Monument

Beaver are an important historic and ecological story in Voyageurs National Park. A skull shows visitors unique adaptations of beaver to their environment.

Voyageurs National Park, Minnesota   Warren Bielenberg

Chellburg Farm, Indiana Dunes National Lakeshore   Warren Bielenberg

An interpreter, dressed as a farmer, shares his life with urban visitors. A theme, such as "Food comes from the farm not the supermarket," gives a "take home" message to this tour.

Courtesy of Jefferson National Expansion Memorial, Missouri

A museum tour should interpret a single theme from selected exhibits. It allows visitors to have more intimate contact with artifacts and to have their questions answered.

Checklist for Trail Interpretation

- **Arrive early** - You should be at the trailhead at least 15 minutes early. First time visitors need assurance that "this is the place."

- **Get to know your participants** - Informal conversations go a long way toward building bridges with your audience.

- **Start on time** - You owe it to the people who came on time.

- **Set expectations** - Distance, what they'll see, and length of time.

- **Make your first stop within sight of your starting point** - Late arrivals can catch up with the group.

- **Stay in the lead** - It should be more exciting to stay with you than to forge ahead on the trail.

- **Keep the visitors comfortable** - Be especially observant of wind and sun in their faces.

- **Go past the object you wish to talk about**, then go back to the middle of the group so all can see it. This is critical in moving efficiently with large groups.

- **Use teachable moments** - If an osprey dives for fish in view of the group, stop discussing pond lilies and focus on the action.

- **Speak loudly but use inflection** - Your voice won't carry as far in the out-of-doors.

- **Return on time** - Whenever possible, bring them back to the beginning point (physically and thematically).

- **Carry a gimmick bag** - All the equipment you might need to help "see things better." It also helps to keep a potential "trouble maker" busy assisting you.

- **Involve the group** -
  - Actions are more meaningful than words.
  - Involve the senses. Smell a milkweed flower; don't just talk about it.
  - Use questioning and discussion as much as telling.

- **Conclude the walk** - Don't allow the group to drift away one by one. Tie the walk to the theme and **end**.

- **Make certain that your activity does not destroy the resource.**

7
Spontaneous Interpretation

...I never met anyone that I couldn't learn something from.
- Warren Wells

Beggich-Boggs Visitor Center at Portage Glacier, Chugach National Forest, Alaska

Donna Zimmerman

Opportunities for interpretation may happen at anytime. Spontaneous interpretation is a natural extension of conversation with visitors. It may take place at information stations or on the site.

Information Stations

Information stations at parks are really "service stations." Imagine pulling off the interstate looking for a service station. You want directions, refreshment, and gasoline. You see an off-brand station, but it is difficult to find the driveway. An inattentive employee, feet propped next to the cash register thumbs through a magazine with greasy hands. A search reveals a dirty bathroom door that is "locked for your protection."

You approach the rumpled, ungroomed body at the cash register. "What highway do I take to get to Indianola?" you ask politely. Without looking up, he nods to a faded map on the wall. You leave, vowing never to return.

Does your information station resemble this scenario in any way?

Make your information station say "You are welcome here. We are here to serve you." It should be visible, well lit, and accessible. Clean bathrooms, maps and brochures should be clearly available. Soft background music offers reassurance in indoor settings. The sight of a uniformed interpreter promises answers to questions.

Information duty is an opportunity to give visitors more than what they came for. You offer visitors a gift of knowledge that will enrich their experience at the site. A well spent moment of your time may live on as a warm memory of the visit. You should look professional, friendly, and approachable. Your grooming and clothing should reflect your agency, not your personal fashion tastes. Be clean, well groomed, and understated.

Be friendly! Respond immediately to an arriving visitor. Make eye contact, smile, and exhibit warm body language. Avoid personal conversations with other employees. Your attention should be focused on the guest.

Anticipate visitor questions about your site and be prepared with complete, but concise answers.

What are the "can't miss" features at your site? Where have people been seeing grizzlies? What is the best time to photograph the canyon? When does the campfire program start? What can I do here in four hours? You can't anticipate all questions, but experience will tell you which ones you must know.

Checklist for Visitor Information Duty

- Look professional.
- Be friendly.
- Respond immediately.
- Focus attention on guest.
- Anticipate questions and be prepared with answers.
- Interpret rules.
- Alert visitors to "can't miss" stories and features.

Studies document that signs and publications are ineffective at communicating rules. The most effective method is person to person contact. Important rules should be explained and a reason given for them. At Denali National Park, it is forbidden to feed ground squirrels that playfully await handouts. When it's explained that large concentrations of these rodents attract grizzly bears, understanding rather than resentment results.

Trail Ridge Visitor Center, Rocky Mountain National Park   Michael Gross
A National Park Service volunteer helps visitors plan a backcountry hiking trip.

Joint National Park Service, Forest Service Visitor Center, Munising, Michigan
Courtesy of Pictured Rocks National Lakeshore
Attention is focused on a visitor seeking information on the Lake Superior region.

Roving Interpretation On Site

Nature is dynamic. Few interpretive programs can completely interpret the ever changing environment. An interpreter patrolling the site can alert visitors to temporary events of great appeal.

You must not only be where events are occurring, but where visitors are found. Position yourself at natural congregation points.

Roving interpreters must know the site and its stories. Look for stories to share with your visitors. Have an interpretive repertoire "in your back pocket" to pull out at appropriate moments.

Photos at right: Chugach National Forest interpreters provide shipboard interpretation on the Alaska Marine Highway. Passengers on these ferries are frequently treated to sights such as glaciers "calving" into the sea, humpback whales surging past the boat, and sea lions leaping from rocks. This is a perfect setting for roving interpretation. Where is your best setting?

Aboard Bartlett, Alaska Marine Highway   Donna Zimmerman

Bartlett   Courtesy of U.S.D.A. Forest Service

Interpreters use the PA system to alert visitors to sightings in Prince William Sound.

Ron Zimmerman

At Corkscrew Swamp Audubon Sanctuary in Florida, interpreters rove the boardwalks. Often they can be found at rest points or overlooks talking with visitors. (Right) The wood stork nesting rookery is a natural congregation point. Information is provided on behavior and breeding success of the birds.

At another point on the boardwalk, a spotting scope focused on a limpkin attracts curious visitors. They then find out more, how limpkins feed only on apple snails, ripping them from the shells with their curved beaks, then snipping out the snail's poison filled gland.

Corkscrew Swamp Audubon Sanctuary, Florida

Michael Gross

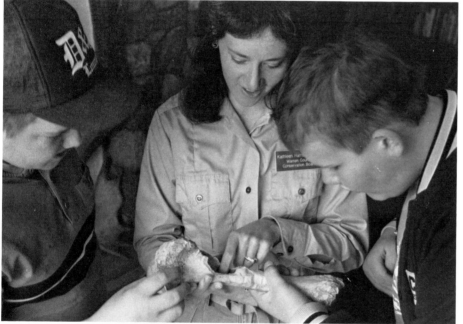

Warren County Conservation Center, Iowa

Paul Regnier

Paul Regnier

Nature centers are ideal for roving interpretation. Visitors handle objects and learn about them from the naturalist. (Left) A rodent-gnawed deer femur teaches ecological interactions. (Above) an owl wing provides a lesson in adaptations for silent flight.

Mesa Verde National Park, NM   Michael Gross

(Left) Roving interpreters answer questions about the Anasazi Indians who lived in these cliff dwellings more than five centuries ago.

Photo by Ron Zimmerman

Courtesy of Harry S. Truman National Historic Site, Missouri

Visitors are greeted at the gate to the Truman home. Historic homes and museums are ideal sites for roving interpretation, adding a human touch.

Callaway Gardens, Georgia   Michael Gross

A costumed interpreter welcomes visitors to a pioneer log cabin museum. She can respond to the particular interests of the visitors.

Warren Bielenberg

Visitors receive individual attention on the Rainey Lake Cruise.

Checklist for Roving Interpreters

- Know the site.

- Know current happenings of interest to visitors.

- Know your visitors and what they are seeking.

- Be concise. Allow your visitor the private experience they are seeking.

- Wear a uniform to identify yourself.

- Be friendly and approachable.

- Use attractants to capitalize on visitor curiosity (scopes, live animals, artifacts).

- Carry props and tools (consult interpreter's knapsack in the appendix).

8 Interpretation for Children

He who would learn to fly one day
must first learn to stand and walk
and run and climb and dance. One
cannot fly into flying.
Nietzche, *On the Spirit of Gravity*

Children make up a large proportion of our visitors. Whether they come with a school, youth organization, or a family, they can provide the enthusiasm and wonder necessary for a successful program.

Special people, places, and experiences from our childhood shape our lives as adults. Lifelong commitments and interests are largely determined by childhood experiences. Interpretation for children can be a vital force for shaping the future.

Warren County Conservation Area, Iowa

Paul Regnier

Child Development for Interpreters

Tilden's fifth principle states *Interpretation addressed to children, (say up to the age of twelve) should not be a dilution of the presentation to adults, but should follow a fundamentally different approach.*

Tilden recognized that children's perceptions and abilities differ from adults'. **It is just as important to recognize that children of different ages have different perceptions and abilities.**

Interpreters need to understand child development if they are to provide age-appropriate interpretation.

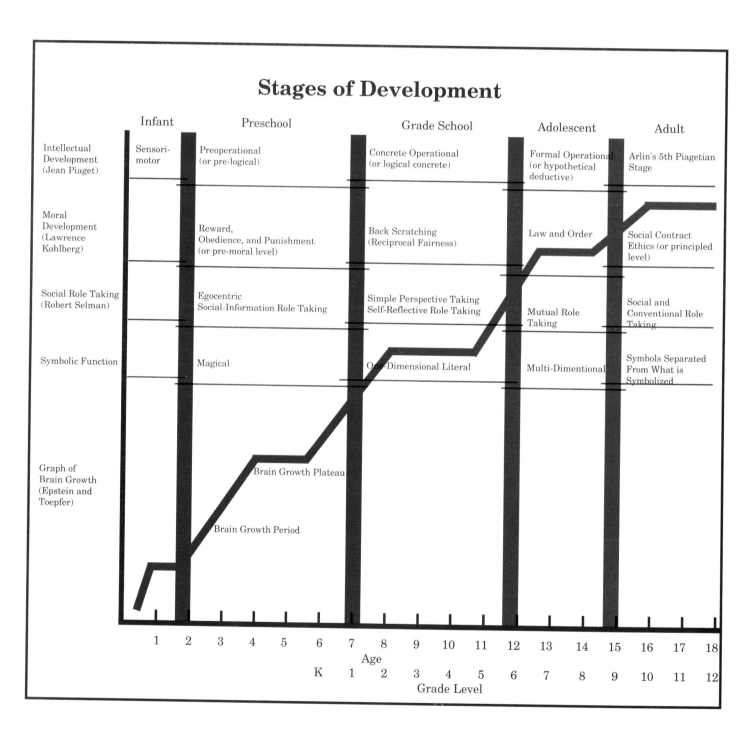

Stages of Development

	Infant	Preschool	Grade School	Adolescent	Adult
Intellectual Development (Jean Piaget)	Sensori-motor	Preoperational (or pre-logical)	Concrete Operational (or logical concrete)	Formal Operational (or hypothetical deductive)	Arlin's 5th Piagetian Stage
Moral Development (Lawrence Kohlberg)		Reward, Obedience, and Punishment (or pre-moral level)	Back Scratching (Reciprocal Fairness)	Law and Order	Social Contract Ethics (or principled level)
Social Role Taking (Robert Selman)		Egocentric Social-Information Role Taking	Simple Perspective Taking Self-Reflective Role Taking	Mutual Role Taking	Social and Conventional Role Taking
Symbolic Function		Magical	One-Dimensional Literal	Multi-Dimentional	Symbols Separated From What is Symbolized
Graph of Brain Growth (Epstein and Toepfer)		Brain Growth Plateau / Brain Growth Period			

Age: 1 2 3 4 5 6 7 8 9 10 11 12 13 14 15 16 17 18

Grade Level: K 1 2 3 4 5 6 7 8 9 10 11 12

Developmental Principles

More than sixty years ago, Jean Piaget observed and cataloged the intellectual development of his children. Over his lifetime, he expanded on these early observations through experiments with children: he would pose simple problems to them and through interviews, analyze how they solved them. His well-known theories of intellectual development were the result.

In recent decades, countless researchers have confirmed and expanded on these early theories. Lawrence Kohlberg examined how moral reasoning evolves. Robert Selman looked at how we assume social roles. Developmental psychologists and their colleagues have given us several principles of development:

- Child development (physical, cognitive, moral, social) is marked by times of noticeable change that is interspersed with times of stability.

- Child development is sequential, i.e., every child passes through a series of distinct stages. Each stage builds on the preceding one.

- Movement from one stage to another is fairly rapid, with most children changing stages at about the same age.

- Movement from one stage to another correlates with brain growth spurts.

- For a variety of reasons (experiential, physiological, sociological), development can be arrested at a lower stage.

- Teaching (and interpretation) must be designed for specific stages of development.

Interpretation for Preschool Children

Interpreters are increasingly being asked to provide programs for preschool children. The lack of extended families, the pursuit of careers by parents, and the increase of single parents have created expectations for many institutions. Parks, nature centers, zoos, and museums are now providing preschool programs which shape attitudes and values at this important early age.

Preschool children are charming, innocent, and eager. To understand this developmental stage, remember these are the years of Santa Claus, a jolly old elf who flies through the air, pulled by eight tiny reindeer, slipping down all the world's chimneys to leave gifts. At about age seven, they suddenly see the illogic of this.

Older siblings take advantage of preschool brothers and sisters. When offered one coin at the candy store and given a choice of a dime or a nickel, preschoolers will take the nickel, not realizing that value is not related to size.

Although they like to be with other children, they tend to play independently. They are very self-oriented. All interpreters have experienced a forest of little hands going up, not to ask a question, but to announce, "My uncle has a pet bird."

Up to about age seven, children see everything in the world as alive. The sun goes to sleep like they do. Puppets are real beings.

Preschool Programs

Preschool programs should focus on play, fantasy, and the senses. Group learning, if done at all, is usually limited to groups small enough to provide individual attention. However, puppet shows, story time, and other programs that engage fantasy, can hold the attention of larger groups for a surprisingly long time.

Effective strategies include:

- Games and play
- Puppets
- Songs
- Stories (told or read)
- Senses exploration

Warren County Cons. Area, IA   Kathleen Regnier
Children explore the world of insects by catching and looking at the real thing and by making insect body parts they can wear.

Warren County Cons. Area, IA   Kathleen Regnier
Smokey Bear is a lovable character who takes children on a nature walk.

Courtesy of Susan Gilchrist, Storyteller
Preschool children love stories. This kindergarten class is listening intently to storyteller Susan Gilchrist, an educator with the Wisconsin Department of Natural Resources.

Jasper County Conservation Area, Iowa   Michael Gross
Colored construction paper is used in sensory exploration. The children search for things in nature that match their colors. Try a box of 64 crayons as a fun alternative.

Interpretation for Grade School Children

Grade school children, especially those in fifth and sixth grade, are the most frequent visitors to nature centers, zoos, and museums. Since they are still in self-contained classrooms, it is easier to take them out of the school than in later grades. These are also the years when participation in youth organizations is highest.

A grade school child has the ability to deal with simple logical relationships. However, reasoning is still dominated by direct personal experience, hence the term "concrete operational."

Early in this stage, the ability to classify objects into categories and to order objects in a series develops. Conceptually, this child is ready to make order out of a complex world. Time relationships become more understandable. Dinosaurs, fanciful reptiles from the past, fascinate them. Classifying for understanding the similarities and differences within and between groups of animals, rocks, plants, or people is a key interest.

Later in this stage, more complex concepts can be understood. A human or a deer can be seen as a member of a complex, interacting community. However, various points of view in complex issues are still difficult. For example, understanding the economic, ecological, and social aspects of the North Slope oil controversy is beyond them. Children at this stage simply cannot manipulate complex sets of variables in their mind.

However, they can reflect on their own behavior and know right from wrong. Simple behaviors - recycling, for example, to "save the earth" are seized upon. Although they may not know the full complexity of the energy crisis, they will badger parents to turn off lights because their teacher told them it was "important to save energy." Subscribing to group norms is important.

Grade School Programs

Grade school programs can be shows for large groups or individual experiences. The critical ingredient is involvement in concrete experiences. In a large group program, group participation can be facilitated by questions from the interpreter and answers from the audience. Physical participation and humor in children's shows is also important.

At Fort McHenry National Historic Site, Maryland, interpreters involve children by "recruiting" them into the army. They must have good teeth to rip the paper cartridge off the musket rounds! "Recruits" are dressed in period uniform and everyone learns how the various items were used.

Metaphors for complex processes are useful at this stage. The Central Wisconsin Environmental Station has an activity called "tree apartments" that compares the forest to an apartment building. "Who lives in the penthouse? Flashy characters like hawks and tanagers that 'drive off in their red Mercedes.' What can we find in the basement (feeling under leaf litter)? Ooooh. Pipes! It's cool! Oh, look at the bugs! I've got bugs in my basement!"

Children's museums have also recognized the need for involvement. Playing with computers, pushing buttons, and manipulating objects are common devices for teaching children about their physical, biological, and sociological world. However, it often requires the help of an adult to get them to think about the idea being demonstrated and not just push buttons to get a reaction.

Effective strategies include:

- Activities and games to teach concepts
- Exploration and discovery
- Sharing and empathizing
- Stories, puppets, skits, and characters
- Questioning strategies
- Devices that can be manipulated
- Physical and sensory involvement
- Metaphors

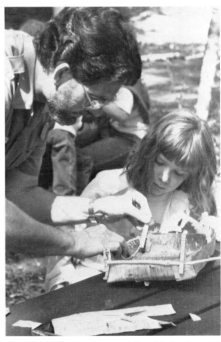

Courtesy of Pictured Rocks National Lakeshore, MI
A Girl Scout program uses traditional crafts to teach about Ojibwa culture. A National Park Service interpreter is assisting a scout with a birch basket.

Warren County Cons. Area, IA   Kathleen Regnier
Catching and observing pond critters is a good way to classify pond life, observe their behavior, and learn how they interact in the pond community.

Jasper County Conservation Area, IA Michael Gross
Seed dispersal is explored by collecting seeds and classifying them by their dispersal mechanism. Wearing wool socks in a field is a great way to snag seeds. Skits are created by the children to express the various kinds of dispersal. The audience has to guess which kind it is.

Everglades National Park, Florida   Michael Gross
A "habitat lap sit" is an involving way to learn about interdependence in nature.

Courtesy of Jefferson National Expansion Mem., MO
Stories about the Lewis and Clark expedition give meaning to the St. Louis Arch.

Warren County Cons. Area, IA   Kathleen Regnier
Children learn about the 19th century fur trade era through stories and by trying on mountain-man clothing.

Warren County Conservation Area, Iowa
Making a birdhouse teaches responsibility for other creatures.
Kathleen Regnier

Warren County Cons. Area, IA   Kathleen Regnier
"Sniffing out a trail" uses natural fragrances to show the significance of odor in nature.

Jasper County Conservation Area, Iowa   Michael Gross
In "making friends with a tree," children are asked to "get to know a tree so well they would recognize it anywhere." After removing their blindfolds, they have to find their tree.

Iowa Conservation Education Center   Michael Gross
"Invent an Animal," an activity exploring animal camouflage, is from OBIS, Outdoor Biological Instructional Strategies. This program was developed by the Lawrence Hall of Science to teach ecology to fifth and sixth graders.

Michael Gross
OBIS is available from Delta Education Inc., Box 915, Hudson, NH 03051, 1-800-258-1302.

Interpretation for Adolescents

Adolescents are approaching the full capabilities of the adult. They can manipulate ideas even when the subject is not present. They can now, for example, begin to weigh the pros and cons of opening up the Alaska North Slope to oil exploration. They can rationally defend a conclusion about the issue and apply it in a broad social context. They can think about the issue in terms of past or future, not just the present. They can contemplate the moral aspects of this issue in abstract and mature ways. They can assume the perspective of others, like Inuit fishermen, oil company executives, or wildlife biologists. Roleplaying is rewarding to them.

Because of physical transformations during this stage, adolescents are at once boisterous and noisy, awkward and self-conscious. They fear looking odd or different. Odd behavior or appearance subjects them to the quick judgment of peers. Peer acceptance is their prime consideration when choosing whether or not to participate in an interpretive program.

Programs for Adolescents

Young people at this age enjoy expressing opinions and assuming adult roles. Rather than reading or telling a story to them, have them read or tell it. Instead of giving a characterization, have them develop and present one.

Simulations and games that explore complex issues or processes allow them to take other viewpoints and discover new ideas. Simulating a congressional hearing on whether or not to open up the North Slope to oil exploration allows them to explore this complex issue from a variety of perspectives. Computer simulations are available on a broad range of topics from ecology to park management.

Exploration and discovery is another involving strategy. A stream exploration, for example, could examine the health of a stream and provide useful input to natural resource management. A supervised archeological dig is an excellent way to explore a past culture.

Effective strategies include:

- Discussion and debate
- Exploration and discovery
- Simulation
- Involvement in activities or projects

Upper Iowa River

Michael Gross

Expeditions help adolescents to learn teamwork, self-reliance, and appreciation of the wilderness.

1

3

2

4

5

The Jasper County, Iowa, Conservation District involves early adolescents in farm related soil and water conservation issues. In a day-long activity, a seventh grade class looks at a watershed to see if the soil is protected from erosion (1). They then look at life in a pond (2) (3) and measure certain chemical aspects (4). They conclude with a report (5) on the water quality of the pond and make recommendations for watershed management.

Photos by Michael Gross

A Checklist for Maintaining Appropriate Behavior

- Set specific behavioral boundaries and expectations early in the program.

- Give problem children something to do (e.g., take responsibility for your props).

- Keep an upbeat attitude - don't yell; yelling confirms that you have lost control.

- Solicit teacher, parent, or chaperone assistance in managing problem children.

- Stand next to problem children, put a hand on their shoulder.

- Model appropriate behavior (e.g., pick up litter).

- Be consistent in handling problems; do not make unenforceable threats.

Working With Schools

School field trips to your site will be most successful if you provide a few essential services.

- Work closely with teachers.

  - Involvement of teachers in planning gives them ownership in the program.

  - Teachers can tell you how a program at your site can enhance their curriculum (look at the curriculum plans for each grade level).

  - Teachers can provide insights on proper teaching strategies.

  - Direct mailings to teachers and presentations at faculty meetings are the best ways to promote your program. Always consult with administrators first.

- Prepare the students for their visit.

  - School children have a need to explore and become comfortable in new settings. Viewing a slide show or video of a site before the visit can greatly speed up this orientation phase.

  - Introduce the "big ideas" of the program prior to the visit. This helps the students learn from the experiences and activities on site.

- Provide an involving program.

  - Organize the class into groups of five to ten, if possible. You may need volunteers.

  - Physical and verbal involvement of the children is essential.

  - Use strategies recommended for various grade levels.

  - Use the resources and stories of the site.

- Follow up the school visit.

  - Help the teachers find ways to use this experience for follow-up learning.

  - Seek feedback from teachers and students. Use their suggestions to improve your program.

9
Gaining Feedback

If interpretation is an art, perhaps it should be
reviewed, just as plays and paintings are.
- Paraphrased from William J. Lewis

Ron Zimmerman

How do you know if your program was successful? Most of us have an intuitive sense of what "worked." Your feelings about a program's success are often a result of complex stimuli and feedback not easily measured qualitatively. Measures such as eye contact, enthusiastic participation, questions, or even relative attendance are all indicators of a program's appeal.

These are immediate, inexpensive, and often accurate means of feedback. Don't be afraid to use them, but don't rely on them totally.

It's also good to get feedback from other sources as well. Totally objective and scientific measures of a program's strengths and weaknesses are often expensive and difficult to obtain, but there are many ways to double check your own "gut" feelings.

Some Methods for Evaluating

- Fill out a self-evaluation checklist.

- Make an audio or video recording of yourself for later review. This can be used for self-evaluation or view with a colleague or "expert."

- Have a colleague observe your presentation and offer suggestions.

- Have an "expert" observe and analyze your presentation.

- Ask your audience. Try an anonymous suggestion box, use a written form, or simply ask selected visitors if the objectives were clear. Did they understand a particular point, what did they like most, etc.

Self-Evaluation

To know if your program was successful, you must have a measure of what "success" is. You must have goals and objectives that you are aiming to achieve and ways of knowing if you actually attained them. So before you begin, state your objectives in terms of something a visitor can do, such as: "After the walk the visitor will be able to tell how jack pine forests are adapted to surviving fires." Obviously, you won't "test" your audience after each walk to make sure they can answer the questions. Objectives will help you "stay on track" and can indicate if you are in touch with your audience.

Here's an example of a simple program plan with a self evaluation.

Program Evaluation:

In your opinion, how successful was the program?

Scale of 1-10 (7) Mostly because the animals were very active. Dividing group into families with young children & those without helped to minimize noise and allowed most interested to stay longer.

What were the program strengths?

Woodcock was very bold and visible in flight. Deer near "peenting grounds" was thrill to all ages. Deb did an excellent intro with "poetic" talk about night smells & sounds.

What improvements would be made in the program plan?

Better timing. We finished 20 minutes late. Hot cocoa wasn't ready back at Visitor Center. Conclusion was not nearly as eloquent as opening... ended in a trailing off not a conclusive "bang."

Types of publicity:

Radio (WSPT, WXYQ)
1 newspaper article
Audubon newsletter

Resource materials/People
Publicity C.

repeat programs:

... am Chair Audubon Chpt.

Schmeeckle Reserve Program Worksheet

Name of Group: Audubon Family Outing   Date: April 16

Time (Length of Visit): 1 hour   # in Group: 37

Interpretor(s): Dick Holmes, Linda Johnson, Jim LeGrande

Site: Visitor Center   Weather: 51° F Cloudy, moist air

Purpose of Visit or Program (What are the group's expectations?):
Sounds of Spring in the Wetlands
Frogs singing
Woodcock courtship?

Theme of the Walk or Program:
"Life begins in Wetlands". Many creatures can only breed in specific wetland areas. Many of these areas are being destroyed or reduced in quality.

Objectives: What will the visitor learn during the program?
That wetlands are valuable breeding areas for many species of birds & frogs. Everyone will be able to I.D. 1. Spring Peepers 2. Wood Frogs 3. Chorus Frogs and tell why they are the 1st to breed in spring

Outline of the Program:
Introduce the Staff & Orient at Visitor Center

Mentor Evaluation

A Good Evaluator Should:

- Not appear unexpectedly.

- Accentuate the positive aspects of a program and be able to build confidence from them.

- Have time to give complete attention to a program and be able to follow up with periodic visits.

- Be prepared to give constructive suggestions and alternatives.

- Have a helpful and unintimidating attitude.

- Be unobtrusive (non-vocal, no uniform).

- Listen to the opinions of the presenter and help him/her to be a better self-critic.

- Limit the number of problems addressed at any one session.

- Help the presenter feel good about being evaluated or at least see the possibilities for growth and improvement.

- Have a two way discussion with the presenter as soon as possible following the presentation.

- Be a good model of interpretive teaching.

Ron Zimmerman

Mentor Checklist

Evaluation forms can be intimidating and impersonal. If used at all, they should be secondary to the dialog between mentor and interpreter. The following guidelines can help you focus on a presentation's strengths and weaknesses.

I. Use of Tilden's Principles

Did the interpreter relate to something within the experience of the audience or involve the audience?

...reveal the essence of the subject rather than simply provide information?

...develop a whole program or only parts and attributes?

...provoke (stimulate, inspire) or simply instruct?

...involve the participants' emotions as well as the intellect (the whole person)?

II. Organization

Did the talk or walk have a stimulating introduction?

Was there a well defined theme?

Was there a good flow (intro-bridge-body-conclusion)?

III. Techniques

Did the interpreter use active language?

...use effective voice inflection and articulation?

...relax the audience and make the talk or walk enjoyable and rewarding?

...have any annoying mannerisms?

...stand in front of the audience and face them?

...maintain contact with the audience?

...warm the audience up to the subject before beginning the presentation?

...involve the audience?

(outdoors)...was the interpreter considerate of the audience (set a reasonable pace, spoke audibly, faced the group away from sun and wind)?

IV. Effort

Did the speaker display enthusiasm and care (props, innovative techniques) in preparing this talk/walk?

Was the presentation an appropriate length?

Was the topic well researched and the presentation practiced?

Visitor Evaluation

A return-addressed, stamped, postcard evaluation form has several advantages over other types of visitor evaluation:

- Visitors feel an obligation to send it back.
- Visitors tend to be more candid in their remarks once they leave the program.
- A postcard response requires little effort.

Front:

Please take a few minutes to help us improve our programs!

Tell us about your visit and yourself.
Dates you visited the park:
_____

Number of people in your family or group who attended this program and their ages:_____

_____

Your residence: city_____

state_____

On the back, please evaluate the program you attended.
Name of program:
_____

Date of program:_____

POST CARD

USA
Stamp

Interpretive Services
Enos Mills Memorial Park
Burwell, NE 68823

Back:

Program Evaluation

I learned little or nothing from this program.
(circle one) Strongly Agree Agree Neutral Disagree Strongly Disagree

I learned a lot from this program.
(circle one) Strongly Agree Agree Neutral Disagree Strongly Disagree

This program was entertaining.
(circle one) Strongly Agree Agree Neutral Disagree Strongly Disagree

This program was boring.
(circle one) Strongly Agree Agree Neutral Disagree Strongly Disagree

The things I liked most about this program were_____

_____

_____

The things I liked least about this program were_____

_____

_____

Resources

Books

These books cover interpretive topics in greater detail than this handbook or present a different perspective. We recommend them.

Roots and Reasons

The Adventures of a Nature Guide
Enos A. Mills
New Past Press, Inc., 2098 18th Ave., Friendship, WI 53934, 1920

Interpreting Our Heritage
Freeman Tilden
University of North Carolina Press, Chapel Hill, NC 27514, 1957

On Interpretation: Sociology for Interpreters of Natural and Cultural History
Gary E. Machlis and Donald R. Field
Oregon State University Press, Corvallis, OR, 1984

Presentation Skills

The Good Guide: A Sourcebook for Interpreters, Docents and Tour Guides
Alison L. Grinder and E. Sue McCoy
Ironwood Publishing, Box 8464, Scottsdale, AZ 85252, 1985

Interpreting for Park Visitors
William J. Lewis
Eastern Acorn Press, Boulder, CO, 1980

Slide Showmanship: How to Put on a Terrific Slide Show
Elinor Stecker
Watson-Guptill Publications, 1515 Broadway, New York, NY 10036, 1987

Environmental Interpretation: A Practical Guide for People with Big Ideas and Small Budgets
Sam H. Ham, North American Press, Golden, CO, 1992

Children's Interpretation

Conservation Seeds Activities Book
Sherri Griffen
Conservation Commission of the State of Missouri, 1984

Hands-On Nature
Jenepher Lingelbach
Vermont Institute of Natural Science, Woodstock, VT 05091, 1986

Hug a Tree
Robert E. Rockwell, Elizabeth A. Sherwood, and Rrobert A. Williams
Gryphon House, Inc., Mt. Rainier, MD 20822, 1983

Reaching for Connections, Vol. 1: Creative Ideas for Enhancing Interpretive and Education Programs
David W. Stokes, Schlitz Audubon Center, 1111 E. Brown Deer Rd., Milwaukee, WI 53217

Reaching for Connections, Vol. 2: Creative Exploration of Nature with Young Children
David W. Stokes, Schlitz Audubon Center, 1111 E. Brown Deer Rd., Milwaukee, WI 53217

Sharing Nature with Children
Joseph Cornell
Ananda Publications, 14618 Tyler Foote Rd., Nevada City, CA 95959, 1979

Sharing the Joy of Nature
Joseph Cornell
Dawn Publications, 14618 Tyler Foote Rd., Nevada City, CA 95959, 1989

Teaching Kids to Love the Earth
Marina Lachecki Herman, Joseph F. Passineau, Ann L. Schimpf, and Paul Treuer
Pfeifer-Hamilton Publishers, 1702 E. Jefferson St., Duluth, MN 55812, 1991

Puppets

The Maher Studios, Box 420, Littleton, CO 80160
A wonderful source of puppet scripts, puppet patterns, puppets themselves and cassette tapes on the "how-to's" of puppetry.

The Interpreter's Knapsack

The following articles from *The Interpreter* offer a potpourri of tools to help you interpret natural and cultural history. The first, by Mike Freed and David Shafer, emphasizes natural history. The second, by Bill Krumbein, emphasizes cultural history.

Gimmicks and Gadgets
Mike Freed and David Shafer
The Interpreter 13(3), 1982.

The Mini-Museum Goes Afield

Gimmicks and Gadgets

Every field interpreter needs tools-an interpretive tool kit composed of gismmicks, gadgets, and goodies which can help create wonder, awe, curiosity, facts, and that special way of seeing. You don't want to forget that certain book, specimen, or instrument that can answer an unexpected question, enhance a special moment, or satisfy the curious student of nature.

Use this list as an idea generator and a checklist for your own interpretive knapsack. What goes in your knapsack will depend on you - your interests, your area - aquatic or desert, wilderness or urban, mountain or coast. You will want to consider the season of the year, the size of your group, and your own area of expertise. Too bad, but not all of these tools will fit on one knapsack!

The Basic Ten - Items commonly encountered in knapsacks.

1. Binoculars and telescope - when you want to be closer to something: a bird, a distant mountain, a star, or a nearby galaxy. Remember, with your naked eye you should be able to see an object in the sky 12 trillion miles away. Do you know what it is and where to look for it?

2. Camera, film, lenses, filters, and other accessories - for creative expression of another kind; for recording, for promoting

interest - if the interpreter thinks it is special enough to photograph, it is probably worth exploring.

3. Hand lens and magnifying glass - the hand lens up to 20X is best for floral identification and viewing small objects, but magnifying glasses, magnifying headsets, and illuminating reading glasses are other tools to enhance the visual senses.

4. Waterproof notebook - for recording ideas, thoughts, and making sketches.

5. Field guides and local keys - birds, mammals, insects, reptiles, amphibians, animal tracks and signs, wildflowers, rocks and minerals, weather, and more. The *Golden Guide* series books are small, inexpensive, and interpretive.

6. Task cards - for directing activities in small groups, for finding and discovering details and hidden beauty. Especially useful for handling large groups. Commercial sets available - OBIS, Sunship Earth, The Green Box, and many more.

7. Twine of string - for web of life game, geologic timelines, relative distances between planets in the solar system, and emergency repairs.

8. Small plastic bags and bottles - for bringing home small treasures or temporarily showing aquatic life.

9. Large plastic garbage bags or litter bags - set a good example or use them in a rainstorm to keep people dry.

10. Small first aid kit or survival kit - safety is the first responsibility of the group leader, but survival can be interpretive, too.

From the Macro to the Micro - to change perspectives, to see more, to become more aware, to enlighten.

11. Bibliography cards - for those interested in further exploration.

12. Photographs - historic photos, seasonal changes, aerials, rare plants and

animals, close-ups including microscope and electron-scanning photos, and other things visitors can't see on their own.

13. Star charts - visitors will enjoy learning how to begin star watching.

14. Cloud charts - weather - it's a cirrus or a stratus - or whether it's not.

15. Skin diver's mask or glass-bottom bucket - for watching the swirling sands at the bottom of a brook, looking into tidepools, etc.

16. Maps - topographic, geologic, vegetation, and historic.

17. Penlight and flashlight - for probing trees and rock cavities, animal burrows, or pond life at night.

18. Pocket mirror - for flashing some sunlight on your subject.

19. Vials with magnifying aids - for many types of small specimens.

For Displaying and Collecting

20. Vials, petri dishes, paper cups - for passing things which might be damaged or injured by direct handling.

21. White bowl or cloth - a contrasting background make it easier to see many small objects.

22. Clear contact paper - for covering specimens to keep for later use.

23. Pins, rubber bands, and thumbtacks - for displaying and pinning specimens.

Other Tools and Gadgets

24. Old dental tools - for probing flowers and other delicate things.

25. Cotton tape measure - comparison of the circumference of trees, measuring.

26. Increment borer - for discussions about the age of trees and factors which affect tree growth.

27. Soil and water thermometers - how much warmer is the lake than the outlet stream water? How well does duff insulate the soil? What is the temperature of compost?

28. White cloth and charcoal - for making rubbings of tombstones, tree bark, and old metal and wood signs.

29. Lightmeter - for comparing light intensity in different environments, for accurate photographic readings.

30. Plaster of Paris and tin cans - for making casts of animal tracks or leaf prints.

31. Flag tape - for temporarily marking things of interest. An alligator clip on one end makes a great clip-on flag.

32. Old toothbrush - gives that agate a new sparkle, cleans a fossil, or brushes up on bones.

33. Small rock samples - when you can't get to the top of a mountain, you can at least show what is up there. Lift a piece of pumice, float it on water, strike with a piece of flint, fool them with fool's gold!

34. Spray bottle - for photographic effects and spiderwebs.

35. Wire net - for dragging the bottom of a stream.

36. Tape recorder - to intensify the auditory senses of your audience. Try playing back territory bird songs and see what happens. Record your observations and notes in the field.

37. Segments of string 100 inches long - for your micro-nature trails. Add toothpicks and voila! A miniature self-guided trail.

38. Small shovel or trowel - soil and plant samples.

39. Collection nets - for airborne or aquatic insects.

40. Red cellophane - for your flashlight on the night hikes and for star gazing. Great for sneaking up on night crawlers.

41. Parabolic reflector - for recording animal sounds in the field.

42. Rock pick or hammer - you can't always judge a rock by its cover.

Still More Gimmicks and Goodies for Naturalists

43. Pocket knife - for opening seeds, prying off bark, or whittling.

44. Litmus paper or soil test paper - for comparing acidity of soils and water in different habitats.

45. Materials for making mushroom prints or preserving spiderwebs - you'll need razor blades, index cards, spray fixative, and paper.

46. Live trap for small mammals.

47. Snare stick or hook - good for picking up snakes or turning over logs or stones.

48. Altimeter - when you are at the top of the world, exactly how high are you?

49. Barometer - looks like a northeaster....

50. Silly putty or modeling clay - when they won't believe rocks can bend, a quick model demonstration can help.

51. Empty slide mount - for composing good pictures.

52. Beuforts' scale of wind force - for estimating wind speed by the motion of tree leaves and branches, chimney smoke, flags, and water waves.

53. Watercolors - India ink, glue and 4 x 6 cards for group poetry, painting pictures, and natural collages.

54. Specimens - liven up your program with a few dead animals. Bring along specimens of insects, fish, reptiles and amphibians, scat, feathers, nests, eggs, skulls, and more.

55. Live animals - one of the most effective tools is life itself. Try a snake, a cricket or other insect, or a mouse.

56. Coffee filters - for filtering life out of pond water.

57. Cotton strips and fingernail polish remover - Crush up leaves and place in a glass container, cover with fingernail polish remover, dangle cotton strips in solution and watch the leaf pigments move up the cotton and separate into different color bands.

58. Masking tape - to tape thumbs for crab and squirrel games and to repair your bulging interpretive knapsack.

59. Tossing rings (hoola hoops) - for plant and soil studies. Throw them in the field - let the area they encircle be your area of discovery.

60. Colored toothpicks - for micro-nature trails and camouflage exercises.

61. Name tags - when you are going to be together for a short while.

62. Hunting or fishing vest - just the thing to have when your interpretive knapsack is full. The myriad of pockets facilitates easy access to often used items.

Last Minute Things You Shouldn't Forget

63. Canteen - to quench someone's thirst, or wish away soil to show fragile roots of a plant.

64. Candy bars and gorp - quick energy on a cold day or on a long hike.

65. Watch - for clocking current speed of streams and to keep track of time. Remember, you can tell time with a compass and find north with your watch, if you know how.

66. Rags - if you want your group to get wet or dirty, make sure they can get cleaned-up, too.

Gosh it never ends. We have a list of many more items, but they don't all fit in the pack or this article. Do you need all these crazy things anyway? Well, maybe just five ore for fun. How about a road kill, or a buffalo chip, empty egg cartons, fish bobbers, toilet paper tubes? How do you think they could be used? We will leave the guessing up to you.

A Gimmicks and Gadgets Potpourri
Bill Krumbein
The Interpreter 14(4), 1983.

Cultural and Historic Interpretive Tools and Gadgets

This list will have many items useful to a naturalist, but special emphasis will be on the items that a historian, archaeologist, or cultural resource specialist could use.

1. A book of Indian legends and myths -- can be used to show how Indians lived in the area, how they viewed the animals and plants, and how their own society relates to ours today.

2. Indian artifacts -- objects like arrowheads, pipes, or other small objects which can be used to exhibit Indian culture. A small leather pouch can work wonders as a carrier of small items.

3. Quotes -- from the journals of explorers of the region.

4. Diaries -- readings from diaries of pioneers and settlers.

5. Xerox copies of old newspaper articles about events in the area.

6. Historic photographs. Cover in plastic or put in a diary notebook for a touch of the past. Please, don't use originals, only copies. Sepia tone adds an extra measure of nostalgia.

7. Tape recordings of sounds like a steam locomotive or other machines of the past.

8. Obsolete implements -- things that have not been used for many years can be a source of interest. Let your visitors guess how the object might have been used.

9. Historic maps -- they show trade, travel, immigration routes, and ghost towns.

10. Raised relief map -- orient visitors to the major landscape features of the area.

11. Oral history tapes and transcripts.

12. Songs reflect a people's way of life. Many hymns, shanties and marching songs tell stories about past ways of life.

13. Puppets -- hand puppets can be easily made and fit into a knapsack. Let the children in your audience be part of the puppet story.

14. Pioneer toys and games. You'd be surprised how many adults in your audience had to make do with inexpensive toys and games. The kids, of course, will love to learn a new cat's cradle or spin the button.

15. Historic bibliography -- a list of books and articles for those visitors who want more detailed information. Be prepared, don't cut their interest short.

16. Costumes -- when introducing local history why not be part of it? Through creative (and historically accurate) use of original and replica clothing, the interpreter can be a Miner 49'er, the school marm, or the Civil War soldier.

17. Food samples -- give the visitor a "taste" of the past. A bit of hard tack or a cup of Mormon tea brings the past to the present.

18. Ball of string -- for making historic timelines.

19. Resource sample -- what brought people to the area originally? Was it gold, silver, timber? Have a sample handy.

20. Petroglyph tracings -- protect a fragile resource such as Indian Petroglyphs by having a copy or tracing made. A tracing also allows visitors to see objects that are too remote, too fragile, or too rare to be seen by the public.

21. Children's books -- the past was not just a bunch of grown-ups. The kids were there too and their toys and books can give us insights into their way of life. Have you looked at McGuffey's Reader recently?

22. Old advertisements -- catalogs, signs, and newspapers. Remember the days when a movie ticket cost a dime? Print 'em up, pass 'em out to your visitors.

23. Artwork -- copies of paintings, woodcuts, and etchings show historical developments.

24. A mat of cedar bark strips woven by Indians -- if you can't have an original garment or basket and you can't afford a good replica, why not a photograph?

25. Political campaign buttons -- to interpret the American political scene.

26. Hand wrought nails with different head types -- to talk about change in the style of nails and how they can be used in dating historical sites.

27. Silver dollars -- they can be used to interpret early silver mining in the western United States. A 20 dollar gold piece or a replica of the gold piece could be used to explain the value of gold then and now.

28. Fragments of old china and bottle glass -- to discuss how these items can be used in dating historical archaeological sites and to trace the trading patterns at the site.

29. Time line charts -- to show the relationship of events. Who was the President of the United States when your local events were taking place? Who was the Czar of Russia, or the King of France?

30. Flip charts with pictures to dramatize events.

31. Knives -- compare different types, and explain cultures or occupations that commonly used each type. The Bowie knife was as famous as the Colt 45.

32. Old letters, old keys, old railroad tickets -- you can add to this list. Think of just one more right now.

33. Butcher paper and charcoal -- used to make rubbings of tombstones and old signs. The rubbings have take-home value for the visitor.

34. Old cameras -- compare them to the modern ones. The old camera is the type early visitors to your site would have used.

35. Models of old buildings - they don't need to be fancy. Make them out of craft items.

36. Courthouse records -- authentic documents can explain deaths, births, mining claims, land deeds, and more.

37. Tools -- gold pans, wood carving implements, and logging equipment make excellent demonstrations. Show the visitor how to split shakes with a mallet and froe.

38. Musical instrument -- a replica of an instrument of the era can add entertainment. If you cannot play it, maybe one of your visitors can.

39. Stone mortar and pestle -- if you don't have an original, try making one and use it to grind grain.

40. Butter churn -- let everyone turn the handle and taste the results.

41. Books of the period -- what works were most popular at a certain time, and what printing styles and techniques were used?

42. Floor plans of buildings -- use them at sites where buildings once stood.

More gimmicks, gadgets, and goodies for the naturalist. (Historians, museum personnel, educators and photographers may like these, too.)

43. Catalogs of outdoor and natural history equipment.

44. Small blackboard.

45. Book or list of geographic names for your area.

46. Infrared detector -- used at night or observing nocturnal animals.

47. Equipment checklist -- when someone asks about your guided hike, be prepared to tell him/her what is needed: wool socks, canteen, etc.

48. Silhouette chart of birds in flight and perched, as in Peterson's Field Guide.

49. Streak plate -- a small square of unglazed porcelain will do the trick. The streak or color of a mineral is often an important means of identifying it. Bring along a sample of *hermatite* for a good demonstration.

50. Caliper -- for comparing the thickness of a leaf versus that of a sheet of paper.

51. Nature magazines -- have a variety so your visitors know what types of publications are available. Give them an index card for writing down information.

52. Magnet -- many rocks and minerals have magnetic properties: see if you can find any. Iron filings on a piece of glass or plastic will display the magnetic field if the magnet is passed under. Why not test for iron in the sand? A compass is also useful for showing the principle of a magnet.

53. Matches -- for safety, for seeing, for experimenting.

54. Gorp -- a combination of raisins, peanuts, Cheerios, M & M's and granola -- use it when your group needs a boost of energy.

55. Gallon glass jars -- a good container for a terrarium or an aquarium, or just temporary quarters for a critter.

56. Feel or touch box -- let your visitors guess the mystery item of the day. The box can be made by lining a milk carton with a heavy cloth. Have an elastic seam near the top for a hand-hole.

57. Peanuts -- have you ever tried eating nuts like squirrels -- that is, without thumbs? Tape your thumbs to your palms and try it.

58. Colored paper -- for demonstrating camouflage ability of certain amphibians.

59. Construction paper and non aerosol spray -- for preserving spider webs as a work-of-art.

60. Mallet, froe, and drawknife -- make cedar shakes, just like in the old days.

61. Tree seedlings -- let your visitors help start a new generation.

62. Pressed and mounted flowers -- lure your visitors back next year when the flowers are in bloom.

63. Fishing bobbers -- for measuring stream flow velocity.

64. Plastic straws -- with a little practice you will learn to impart a gentle breeze to delicate objects like a flower or seedhead.

65. Products derived from plants -- dyes are an example, or jojoba oil or mint oil.

66. Single edge razors -- for peeling, slicing, and splicing. For example, try finding the algal layer within a lichen.

67. Organic compounds are the active ingredient for certain colors from plants. Check with a chemist. Bring along a sample.

68. Cross sections of agates and other stones.

69. Chalk -- if you are in an area with slate, remind your visitors of the days when blackboards were really made from slate.

70. Vials of sand -- for miniature rock gardens.

71. Antler from a buck -- demonstrate to your visitors what "4-point" is.

72. Goggles -- a good safety item, especially when using a rock hammer. Can be used in sand or dust storms to interpret desert adaptations. Can be used underwater.

73. Rain gauge -- how wet did we get on our hike today?

74. Styrofoam boards -- for mounting and displaying insects.